THE LION BOOK OF
STORIES OF JESUS

Retold by Timothy Dudley-Smith
Illustrated by Terry Gabbey

A LION BOOK
Oxford · Batavia · Sydney

Contents

Published by
Lion Publishing plc
Sandy Lane West, Oxford, England
ISBN 0 85648 906 9
Lion Publishing Corporation
1705 Hubbard Avenue, Batavia, Illinois 60510, USA
ISBN 0 85648 906 9
Albatross Books Pty Ltd
PO Box 320, Sutherland, NSW 2232, Australia
ISBN 0 86760 612 6

First edition 1971 published by Falcon Books
under the title *A Man named Jesus*
This edition 1986
Reprinted 1987, 1988, 1990, 1991

British Library Cataloguing in Publication Data
Dudley-Smith, Timothy
   [A man named Jesus]. The Lion book of stories
of Jesus.
   1. Jesus Christ–Biography–Juvenile literature
   I. Title   II. The Lion book of stories of Jesus
   232.9'01   BT302
   ISBN 0 85648 906 9
   ISBN 0 86760 612 6 Australia

Printed in Italy

About this book

The life of Jesus Christ has long been known as 'the greatest story ever told'; and this book is therefore as much for families as for children. The stories are written with an ear to their being read aloud together, though the design and colourful presentation of the book will also attract children who want to read it for themselves.

These forty-four short episodes make good bedtime reading, perhaps as part of a child's prayers; and with one story a day, the whole outline of the life of Jesus unfolds in a few weeks. Some of the events will already be familiar, but a regular reading links them together so that they are no longer isolated and unrelated incidents, but combine to present an accurate picture of Jesus Christ in his life on earth. Indeed, these stories have already proved popular beyond the family circle, in schools and Sunday schools and wherever – children like to hear stories read aloud.

A distinguishing mark of the book is the way it is rooted in the Bible, especially the Gospel of Luke. Imagination has been used, of course; but carefully controlled by what we know from the Gospels, by our knowledge of the time, and by established Christian tradition. No named characters have been invented and very little dialogue. The words of Jesus, in particular, are largely drawn from established translations of the Bible in common use. This account, therefore. although simplified and imaginatively presented, is still the authentic story as we have it in the Gospels, an essential part of every child's spiritual inheritance.

If families who begin with these stories will later go on to read the Gospels together, perhaps in a modern translation, that will be best of all.

Timothy Dudley-Smith

The Road to Bethlehem

Clip-clop, clip-clop, slowly the donkey plodded forwards. Joseph walked beside him holding the bridle, trudging through the dusty twilight. It had been a long day and a long journey – but there at last were the roofs of Bethlehem.

Joseph must have found it all a little strange – wonderful, of course, but strange just the same. Perhaps his thoughts went back to that night, months ago now, when first the angel of God had spoken to him in a dream and told him that his wife Mary was to have a son. In those days sons were often named after their fathers or their grandfathers; but the angel had said 'No'. The son God was sending to Mary and Joseph was to be named Jesus (which means Saviour) because,

said the angel, 'he shall save his people from their sins'.

Mary too had had a visitor. The angel Gabriel, one of God's heavenly messengers, had come to stand beside her bed one night.

'Do not be afraid,' Gabriel had said. 'God loves you dearly. You are going to be the mother of a son, and you will call him Jesus. He will be great and will be known as the Son of God Most High. He will be King over Israel for ever; his reign shall never end.'

The donkey stumbled on the stones. Joseph glanced up at Mary and she smiled back – not far to go now. Really, thought Joseph, she shouldn't be making this journey; the baby would come very soon. But the government had ordered everyone to make the journey to the place of their birth to be counted and registered and to pay their taxes. So here they were.

Bethlehem was noisy and full of people. They had nowhere to sleep, and there was no room at the inn; every corner was full of visitors who had come for the registration. The best they could do at last was to find – very thankfully – a stable with an empty stall. The clip-clop ceased. Mary and Joseph, and no doubt the donkey too, would have a bite of supper.

And there was one thing more. By the light of the tiny lantern Mary found an empty manger, the wood old and worn, but solid and strong. She and Joseph filled it with the cleanest of the straw, and then there was nothing left to do. The noise of the town died away. Only Mary and Joseph watched and waited, holding hands in the darkness while the oxen munched and snorted in the stalls nearby.

God and his angels kept watch over the darkened stable. It was Christmas Eve.

From Luke's Gospel, chapters 1 and 2

7

Christmas Day

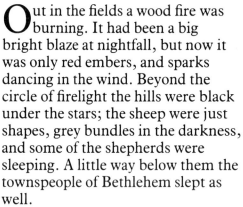

Out in the fields a wood fire was burning. It had been a big bright blaze at nightfall, but now it was only red embers, and sparks dancing in the wind. Beyond the circle of firelight the hills were black under the stars; the sheep were just shapes, grey bundles in the darkness, and some of the shepherds were sleeping. A little way below them the townspeople of Bethlehem slept as well.

Suddenly – more suddenly than you can imagine – an angel of the Lord appeared among the startled shepherds. Light burst upon them, blazing with the glory of God and the brightness of heaven. The shepherds gazed wide-eyed and open-mouthed, motionless with terror.

'Do not be afraid,' said the angel. 'I bring good news. Today in Bethlehem a Saviour has been born for you. He is . . .' (and perhaps there was a moment's pause while the world waited) 'He is . . . Christ, the Lord. And this is your sign,' went on the angel, 'you will find a baby lying in a manger.'

And all at once the night sky above them was full of singing angels, praising God and saying:

'Glory to God in highest heaven,
and on earth peace for men
on whom his favour rests.'

And then once more the shepherds were alone. Darkness and silence settled again upon the hills. The fire crackled softly and a sheepbell tinkled. No one spoke or moved. Later – it must have seemed much later – the shepherds found themselves hurrying together down the path towards the town. 'A child in a manger,' they thought; and the place to look for a manger is a cowshed or a stable.

Perhaps it was Mary's lantern that brought them to the doorway in the hours before the dawn. All her life long Mary must have remembered those first visitors to her new baby – rough, bearded weather-beaten faces, patched cloaks and stout staffs, strong hands huge beside baby hands, and eyes still full of the angel's glory and the radiance of heaven.

Soon dawn came to Bethlehem, and then full day. There were no cards and no presents, no decorations, no special food. But there was good news, singing and great joy, and the birth of Jesus.

It was a very happy Christmas!

From Luke's Gospel, chapter 2

Wise Men from the East

Clearly, they had come a long way. You could see that from their luggage, their jars and pouches, leather bags and wicker baskets; and from their strange clothes and high-boned foreign faces. Even their camels were somehow different from the ordinary camels of Jerusalem.

'Special, they are,' the innkeeper where they lodged might say to his friends. 'Kings, I wouldn't wonder; scholars and stargazers from the lands of the east; and wise, mark you, wise as wise.'

It was true what the innkeeper said. The strange foreign visitors were indeed wise men from the east. They had seen a new star in the night sky, far away in their own country. According to their books and legends it was the sign of a king's birth – a very great king indeed – in far-off Judea. The star called them to leave their homes and make the journey and find the king; and they had precious gifts in their saddlebags.

Travel-worn and tired, they had come at last to the country of Judea, and the city of Jerusalem, where Herod reigned as king.

Now King Herod was old and very cruel. He knew nothing, and his courtiers knew nothing, of the birth of any other king nearby. But when he summoned statesmen and advisers, they told him of an ancient promise in the scroll of the prophet Micah that the King of Israel would be born in Bethlehem, just a few miles away.

Herod was cunning as well as cruel. He told the wise men how to get to Bethlehem and sent them on their way.

'When you have found your new king,' he said to them, 'come back and tell me, so that I may go myself and worship him.' But in his wicked heart he planned to kill the child when the wise men had found him, and so be free of any rival to his throne.

So the wise men set off on their camels to ride the few miles south to

Bethlehem. The star which they had seen in the east still went in front of them, until at last it shone directly over the house where Mary and Joseph were lodging with their little son. The foreigners dismounted, entered with grave solemn courtesy, and fell on their knees to worship Jesus. They had found the king they had come so far to seek.

One by one they opened their treasures, and gave to Mary the gifts they had brought for him: gold, precious and glinting in the lamplight; and spices, filling the little room with the heavy fragrance of frankincense and myrrh.

They left as mysteriously as they came; but they did not go back to tell King Herod. God warned them in a dream that Herod was not to be trusted, and so they set off home without returning to Jerusalem.

But among the little shirts and clothes and blankets Mary kept for Jesus, there remained the strange rich gifts by which she would always remember them – yellow gold, sweet-smelling frankincense, and bitter myrrh.

From Matthew's Gospel, chapter 2

The Refugees

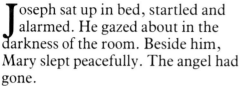

Joseph sat up in bed, startled and alarmed. He gazed about in the darkness of the room. Beside him, Mary slept peacefully. The angel had gone.

For a moment Joseph sat still, thinking hard. It must have been a dream then, he thought to himself, but a very vivid one. An angel of God had stood in that very room, and spoken to him. It was not the first time, of course. An angel had spoken to Joseph in a dream once before, to tell him that Mary would have a son – and in time Jesus had been born. But now the angel had brought very different news.

'King Herod is going to search all Bethlehem,' the angel warned him. 'He wants to find Jesus and kill him. Get up at once, and take the child and his mother, and escape with them to Egypt. Stay there until I tell you it is safe to return.'

Mary stirred in her sleep as Joseph shook her gently but urgently by the shoulder. Then, in a moment, she was wide awake as Joseph told her his dream. They knew what they had to do.

Not long after, in the darkness of the street, a door creaked open. Joseph and Mary stole silently out of the house together, and long before cockcrow they had left the town behind them, and were hurrying southward on the road to Egypt. Joseph carried the luggage, and Mary the baby. Whenever she thought of

King Herod and his soldiers she would clutch Jesus closer to her in the cold morning air, and pray in her heart that God would protect them all. Egypt was an unknown country. They would be among strangers and far from home. But at least they would be safe.

So they journeyed for three or four days, picnicking by the roadside, and sleeping wherever they could find shelter, until they came to the bank of the great river. Beyond lay a new country, and a new life.

They had left Bethlehem not a day too soon. Herod, furious because the wise men had tricked him, sent his soldiers to the town with orders to kill every little boy under two years old. But for the angel's warning, Jesus would have been among them.

Once in Egypt, Joseph and Mary found a place to live, where Joseph could work as a carpenter because that was his trade. For a time at least their travels were over. Jesus grew bigger and stronger, like other little children, and Mary would watch him running and playing in the sunshine, and wonder if he would ever see the home they had left behind in Galilee.

And then one night the angel came again, to tell them that Herod was dead, and it was safe to go home. Soon after that they began yet another journey, pressing on hour after hour through the dust and stones of the road, until they began to recognize the shapes of their familiar hills and found the little green valley that would bring them to Nazareth.

At long last, Jesus was home.

From Matthew's Gospel, chapter 2

Lost in Jerusalem

It was all wildly exciting! Last year, and the year before, and the year before that, Jesus had waved goodbye to his parents when they set out on their annual visit to Jerusalem. Then he had had to wait two whole weeks, looked after by relations and friends, until their return. But this year, this wonderful year, he was going with them. This year he was twelve years old.

When they left home that morning, half the village seemed to be on the road, making their way to Jerusalem for the festival. Mary had often told Jesus of the great city of Jerusalem, and about the magnificent Temple (where he had been carried as a tiny baby, too young to be able to remember) and about the Feast of the Passover which came round with every spring. It was springtime now, and the white path through the cornfields was bordered with the red and blue and purple of the wild flowers.

To Jesus, Jerusalem was all that he had hoped for. He loved the crowds and the bustle, the markets and the people, the busy streets and passageways. He saw the white-robed priests and the burly Roman soldiers, the great houses and the open spaces – and here was the Temple, huge and splendid behind its walls and battlements.

As the days of the festival went by, Jesus and his parents were often in the Temple. He came to know the courts and gateways, the steps and passages, and the great marble columns. To the boy from the country all Jerusalem was wonderful; but the Temple with its wise old priests and teachers seemed somehow to be like another home.

At last the day came to set off on the journey back to Nazareth. Mary and Joseph, and a whole party of friends, were to travel together; and they had a lot to talk about. Jesus was nowhere to be seen, but his parents were not surprised. He was sure to be in one of the other parties, with friends of his own age. But at nightfall, when supper was ready and there was still no sign of him, they began to be anxious. They went from group to group, asking for him. No one had seen him all that day's journey. He was lost.

How worried Mary and Joseph must have been! Next day, while all the others journeyed on towards home, they retraced their steps back to Jerusalem. For two whole days they looked for him, asking here, searching there, but no one had news of their son.

And then on the third day, as they were wandering anxiously through

the Temple, they saw a boy of twelve surrounded by a group of teachers. It looked very like . . . Could it be . . .? Yes! It was Jesus.

Mary spoke first: 'My son,' she said, 'why have you treated us like this? Your father and I have been looking for you everywhere.'

And Jesus said to her, 'But why were you looking for me? Did you not know that I was bound to be in my Father's house?'

Later – years later – Mary would come to understand more of her son, and what he meant by this reply. For the moment it was enough that they had found him, and he was safe. Thankfully the reunited family set off again for Nazareth and home.

From Luke's Gospel, chapter 2

Jesus and John

Only the river was cool that day. It flowed quietly along, in no great hurry, at the bottom of the valley. The sun beat down, and because the valley was sheltered from the wind, it grew hotter and hotter. Yet still the people came.

They came to the riverside – the River Jordan was its name – to listen to a man called John. He stood by the bank of the river, and every day he preached to the crowd.

Those at the front could see him clearly, a wild stern-looking man, burnt brown with the sun and wind, and thin from long days in the desert with very little food. He talked – and somehow you had to listen – he talked of a new kind of kingdom, the Kingdom of heaven; and his words made all who heard him search their hearts, and remember uncomfortably the wrong things they had done and the dark and shabby corners in their lives. And he told the people to be on the look out for someone else, another preacher who was still to come, greater than any other, a man of God.

Every now and again John would stop preaching and would baptize people. They came forward, persuaded by his words, and waded out with him into the river. There he poured water over them, or dipped their whole bodies down under the water, as a sign that they were sorry for their sins and wanted to be washed clean again and to make a new start. And because the crowds came to hear

him, and he was always baptizing, they called him John the Baptizer, or John the Baptist.

One day, Jesus came to him at the River Jordan.

For eighteen years, since that visit to Jerusalem at the age of twelve, Jesus had been living quietly at home with his family at Nazareth. He learned the trade of a carpenter in his father's workshop. He helped his parents bring up his younger brothers and sisters. Now he was thirty years old. It was time for Jesus to set out on his travels, teaching and preaching about God.

But first he came to John. John the Baptizer looked at him and saw a man from Galilee, young and strong, not outwardly different from many others. Then he looked again, and recognized him, and he knew in his heart who Jesus was. He took a step back. 'Do *you* come to *me*?' he asked. 'It should be the other way around; I need to be baptized by you.'

But Jesus convinced him that it was right, and John at last agreed. They went together into the river, and there Jesus was baptized. And as he came out, dripping wet and with the cool water running off him, he saw the heavens opened and the Spirit of God coming down like a dove upon him.

And a voice from heaven said, 'This is my Son, my beloved, in whom I am well pleased.'

And Jesus left John, and the river, and the crowds, behind him; and went into the desert to be alone with God.

From Matthew's Gospel, chapter 3, Luke's Gospel, chapter 3

In the Desert

From the cool river and the noise of the crowd, Jesus went by himself into what they called the wilderness. This was a desert place, not the flat and sandy kind of desert, but bare and rocky and dry. A few wild animals – perhaps even a few lions – lived there, but no one else. At midday, in the glare of the sunlight, all was still, nothing moved. There were no trees, no streams, no people; only the heat and the rocks and the silence.

For six weeks Jesus lived in this desert, seeing no one and with nothing to eat. By day in the shadow of a cave, at night alone under the stars, in silence and solitude, Jesus thought and prayed, and talked to his heavenly Father. And alone in that desert he met and fought with the devil, God's enemy, Satan the evil one, in three great temptations. More than anything in the world, Satan wanted Jesus to make a wrong choice; to put his own comfort or convenience above his Father's will.

Satan knew that by this time Jesus was very hungry. It was weeks since he had had a meal.

'If you are really the Son of God,' said Satan, 'you need not go hungry. Tell these stones to turn into loaves of bread.'

It would have been easy for Jesus to agree; it would not have done anyone any harm; he had only to say the word. But Jesus would not be tempted to use his powers simply to please himself. Instead, he answered, 'The Scripture says, "Man shall not live by bread alone, but by every word of God".'

Satan had no answer to that; so he tried again. He stood with Jesus high above the city of Jerusalem, perched on the topmost ledge of the great Temple building. Far, far below them, the people seemed no bigger than flies, crawling about the narrow streets.

'If you really are the Son of God,' said Satan again, 'then jump. Throw yourself down. For the Scripture says that God will command his angels to protect you; and they will see you come to no harm.'

But Jesus would not be tempted to force his heavenly Father to prove his words.

He answered Satan, 'Scripture says again "You are not to put the Lord your God to the test".'

Satan tried a third time. They stood together on a mountain-top, and saw all the kingdoms of the world spread out below them in a moment of time.

'I will give you all that you see,' said Satan to Jesus, 'with its power and its glory. It is all mine, and it shall be yours *on one condition*. All you need to do is kneel at my feet and worship me.'

But Jesus would not be tempted to bargain with Satan. For the third time he answered with the words of Scripture.

'Away with you, Satan,' he said. 'For it is written, "You shall worship the Lord your God and Him alone".'

And with that, Satan gave up and went away. Three times he had tempted Jesus, and failed each time. The struggle was over for the moment. So Jesus was left in peace; and God sent angels to look after him.

From Matthew's Gospel, chapter 4, Luke's Gospel, chapter 4

Andrew and Simon

It was still quite early, and a fine sunny morning. The Sea of Galilee (which is not really a sea but a huge inland lake) lay blue and calm, little waves lapping the sandy shore, and the hills across the water faint in the haze.

Andrew's busy fingers worked at the net before him, untwisting the tangles of the night's work, and knotting new twine into broken meshes. He and his brother Simon – he glanced across at Simon working on another net nearby – had fished all night and caught nothing. The lake could be like that sometimes. Perhaps at dusk they would try again . . .

As he worked at the net, Andrew listened. He and Simon, and their partner John, had already begun to be disciples of Jesus. They had met him first in Jerusalem during Passover week; and found that he, like themselves, also came from Galilee.

Since then they had often talked with him here by the edge of the lake. There was something about him which drew people to him.

Andrew was listening to Jesus now. Quite a crowd had gathered to hear him – fishermen and traders and passers-by – and Jesus was hemmed in on all sides as they pressed to get near him at the water's edge.

As Andrew watched, Jesus turned from the crowd and spoke quietly with Simon for a moment. Simon nodded, and he began to run the fishing boat down from the beach into

the shallow water. Andrew left his net in a hurry, and ran to jump in beside them. And so from the boat, lifting a little to the waves, Jesus preached to the people on the shore. Andrew sat and listened, glad that their boat was proving useful to the Master.

Presently Jesus finished speaking, and the crowd began to drift away. Simon and Andrew started to bring the boat to shore, but Jesus stopped them.

'Push out into deep water,' he said to them, 'and let down your nets for a catch.'

Simon told him how they had fished all night and caught nothing. 'But if you say so,' he added, 'I will let down the nets.'

And so, offshore where the water ran deep, they tried again. It was plain from the moment they started to haul the nets that they had a record catch. The nets began to break under the strain, and they had to signal to John and his brother James to come and help them. Eventually they filled both boats to sinking point with the weight of fish.

Simon was quite overcome, and fell on his knees before Jesus. 'Keep away from me, Lord,' he said, 'I'm only a sinful man.'

But Jesus said to him, 'Do not be afraid, Simon. From now on you will be catching *men*.'

When they had brought the boats to shore, the four fishermen, Simon and Andrew and James and John, left everything to follow Jesus.

From Matthew's Gospel, chapter 4, Luke's Gospel, chapter 5

9

Village Wedding

The room looked beautiful. Beneath the high ceiling the long table stood laden with food and wine for the wedding guests. The lamps and candles shone brightly in the still evening air, and round the table were chairs and couches (some of them borrowed from friends) covered in soft cushions and rugs and tapestries. It was the very best the village of Cana could provide.

Cana was not far from Nazareth, and Mary was among the special guests who had been asked to the wedding. When it was known that Mary's son Jesus was back home with her for a few days, he and his friends were invited too.

And soon the bride and groom were husband and wife, the wedding ceremony was over, and the feast was in full swing.

Halfway through the evening one of the helpers came in from the kitchen, looking very worried.

He whispered in Mary's ear. She got up from her seat and followed the servant out of the crowded room, beckoning to Jesus to join her outside. There they found the servants standing about helplessly holding empty wine-jugs. The feasting was not half over, but all the wine was finished. It would be a terrible disgrace in front of so many guests.

Mary turned to Jesus. 'They have no wine left,' she said.

The servants looked from one to the other, from Mary to Jesus and from Jesus to Mary. They could not understand what she was asking, or why he said to her, 'My time has not yet come'.

But Jesus' face told Mary what she wanted to know. She turned towards the waiting servant and said briskly, 'Do whatever he tells you.'

Jesus pointed to six very large stone water jars standing nearby. They had held water for the guests to wash with when they first arrived and now they were empty.

Jesus said to the servants, 'Fill the jars with water.' They were puzzled, but they did as they were told.

When all six jars were full to the brim with water from the well (and by that time the guests were wondering why the servants were so long refilling the wine jugs) Jesus gave orders to fill the jugs from the water jars and take them to the Steward of the Feast. The Steward was the man in charge of the festivities. And this too the servants did.

It was water that they had put into the six big jars; but it was wine that they poured into the Steward's cup. He took a sip, and then another, and looked with a new respect at the wine before him. He called down the table to the bridegroom and said, 'Everyone usually serves the good wine first and keeps the poor stuff for later on. But this is the very best that you've kept back till now!'

Not the Steward of the Feast, nor the guests, nor even the bridegroom knew the secret of the wine. But Mary knew, and the servants who filled the wine jars; and so later did Jesus' friends. It was the first of the signs by which Jesus began to show them who he was, and lead them to believe in him.

From John's Gospel, chapter 2

10

A Windy Night

It looked like the right house, though it was hard to be sure in the darkness. With his hand raised ready to knock, the visitor paused. He looked left and right along the windy street but there was no one else about – that was one thing to be thankful for. Doubts nagged at his mind. What would his friends say if they knew that he, Nicodemus, one of the leading men in the city, had walked halfway across Jerusalem on a cold spring night, to talk to Jesus?

'*Jesus of Nazareth?*' they would ask in biting tones. 'Do you mean that fellow who caused such an uproar in the Temple? He must have been mad from all accounts, charging through the courtyards with a whip in his hand, driving out the stall-holders and money-changers. Disgraceful, I call it. He was lucky not to get hurt.'

Standing hesitant on the doorstep, Nicodemus made up his mind. He wanted to know the truth about God, and he believed this young teacher from Galilee could help him. It had been the act of a brave man and an honest one to clear the Temple of traders – the act of a man who knew that God was with him. Nicodemus lifted his hand a second time, and knocked softly on the bolted door.

He was shown into an inner room, with a lamp burning on the table. Jesus rose to greet him, and they sat down.

'Master,' began Nicodemus, 'we realize that you are a teacher sent by God. No one can do these signs that you do unless God is with him.'

'Believe me,' said Jesus, 'unless a man has been born again, he cannot see the Kingdom of God.'

'But how can a grown-up man be born?' asked Nicodemus. 'Can he go back inside his mother and be born a second time?'

Jesus explained that he was not speaking of the beginning of human life when a baby is born; but about God's life which he wants people to have.

'Flesh can give birth only to flesh,' Jesus told Nicodemus. 'It is spirit that gives birth to spirit. Do not be surprised when I tell you that you must be born again. The wind blows where it likes. You can hear the sound of it, but you have no idea where it comes from or where it goes. Nor can you tell how a man is born by the wind of the Spirit.'

Nicodemus hung on Jesus' words, his eyes puzzled and his brow furrowed, trying hard to understand. They talked on into the night, and Jesus told Nicodemus many things. Some of them he would only understand in years to come. But out of their talk that night was forged a single sentence – twenty-eight short words – which sums up the heart of what Jesus had to say. It is there for anyone to read, like the rest of this story, in chapter three of the Gospel of John:

'God loved the world so much that
he gave his only Son, so that
every one who has faith in
him may not die but have
eternal life.'

Nicodemus had plenty to think about as he hurried home through the windy dark. Many things about their talk had puzzled him. There was much he did not understand. But he was sure of this: Jesus, the young teacher from Nazareth, was no ordinary man.

From John's Gospel, chapter 3

Down from the Roof

The news was everywhere. The shopkeepers were full of it and told their customers. Down by the shore the fishermen had heard it; they talked to one another as they sorted the catch.

'Have you heard the news?' they asked. 'Jesus is back again, here in Capernaum. This morning he's going to go on with his teaching, and tell some stories. Hurry along now, and get the work finished, and we'll all go and hear what he has to say.'

The news had even reached a dark little room at the back of the village where there lived a paralyzed man. For a long time now he had lost the use of his legs. He lay all day on a mattress, and could not move from his bed unless his friends carried him. All Capernaum knew that he would get no better, and never walk again.

'Jesus,' he thought to himself. 'He's the teacher who heals sick people. He cured that poor woman with fever; and the man in the synagogue with the evil spirit; and they do say that he put his hand on a man with leprosy and made him well and whole. Ah, Jesus,' he said to himself, 'I wonder if you could do anything for my poor legs?'

Just then there was the sound of running feet outside the window. Through the doorway, hot and breathless, burst four excited men, who all began to talk at once.

'Have you heard . . .?' asked the first.

'Jesus is here . . .' said the second.

'We thought we'd come round . . .' added the third.

'. . . and carry you to see him,' said the fourth.

And with that, they stood one at each corner of the bed, and lifted the mattress like a stretcher, with the paralyzed man still lying on it. Between them they carried him out into the sunlight, and down the hill to the house where Jesus was.

There was a crowd in the street outside, quite blocking the doorway. Inside, too, the house was packed with people. There was no hope of getting in. But the four friends had an idea. They whispered together, and then carried their stretcher round to the back of the house, and very carefully up the steps onto the flat roof. The roof was made of mud and plaster, on wooden beams; and, putting down the stretcher, the four men began to dig.

Down below, all unsuspecting, the crowd stood and listened to Jesus. Suddenly, a little shower of earth fell from the roof. A shaft of bright dusty sunlight appeared. Jesus stopped speaking and looked up. The whole room watched (and the householder very anxiously, because it was his roof!) as the hole grew bigger. Presently the stretcher, with a rope at each corner, swayed down to land at Jesus' feet.

Jesus looked for a long moment at the paralyzed man. He needed

strength for his poor thin legs, and forgiveness for his sins. 'My son,' said Jesus, 'your sins are forgiven.'

Some of the very religious people were shocked by this. 'Who does he think he is, to talk of forgiving sins?' they asked themselves – and Jesus knew just what was in their minds.

'Which do you suppose is easier,' he asked them, 'to say to a paralyzed man "Your sins are forgiven," or to say "Get up, pick up your bed and walk"? But to show you that the Son of Man has the right on earth to forgive sins' – and here Jesus turned to the paralyzed man lying on the floor beside him – 'I say to you, "Stand up, pick up your bed, and go home."''

And that is just what the man did. He found he could move his legs; he could put his feet to the floor; he could stand. Watched by his excited friends from their hole in the roof, he picked up his mattress . . . and *walked!* The crowd parted as he moved towards the door. They were astonished and amazed. They had never seen anything like it. But then they had never before met anyone like Jesus.

From Luke's Gospel, chapter 5

The Tax-collector

The long table by the roadside was all but empty now. Matthew scooped up the piles of coins paid by the last people to travel that way, counted them with an experienced eye, and dropped them into the open money bag. He tied the string of the bag, straightened his aching back, and looked with distaste at his hands. He had washed them at midday; but now they were stained and grimy, smelling of copper and the greasy leather of the money bags. There were many things about his job Matthew disliked, and the dirt on his hands was only one of them – for Matthew was a tax-collector.

In those days, to be a tax-collector was to have few friends. The taxes were harsh, often unfair, and a great burden on poor people. They felt the taxes they had to work so hard to pay were not even for the good of their own country, but went straight to the pockets of rich foreigners in Rome. So they feared and despised the tax-collectors. Ordinary decent people wanted nothing to do with them.

Matthew's office, which was a sort of Custom's House as well, stood beside the busy road that ran by the shore of the Sea of Galilee. White-sailed boats ferried to and fro across the lake; and some of their cargo would be taxed. So would some of the people, with their camels and their donkeys, who passed continually along the road. Many people found

their way to the waterfront; and Matthew had often noticed Jesus among them. Jesus liked to teach here by the lakeside, where there was always a crowd ready to listen; and Matthew sometimes found time to listen too.

Today it was spring. Matthew looked again at his grubby hands and sat down wearily beside his table. These long afternoons were very tiring. He still had several hours on duty before it was time to go home.

And just then, among the passers-by, he caught sight of Jesus himself.

Jesus stopped. He recognized the tax-collector as one who had often joined the edge of the little crowd that gathered to hear his teaching. Perhaps he saw something in Matthew's face that suggested he was ready to know more. Their eyes met as Jesus looked at him. He saw the sadness in his eyes, the stained hands, the stooping back, bowed from much bending over the long table and the ledgers. Then Jesus spoke.

'Follow me,' he said.

Matthew was ready. Many things had prepared him for this moment, and he recognized it when it came. He stood up, and like a man putting all his past behind him, he came out from behind his long table with never a backward look, and walked away in Jesus' company, a happy man.

From Luke's Gospel, chapter 5

On the Hillside

The last light of day had almost gone. Jesus had been walking steadily uphill for the last half hour, but now he stopped and looked back. It was almost too dark to make out the sheep-track he had been following, but down below in Capernaum a few lamplit windows shone like yellow stars. High above him the paler stars of evening glittered in the sky.

At last beside the pathway Jesus found just the place he wanted: a fold in the hillside, sheltered and out of the wind, a patch of turf and a level rock. There, all that night, until the stars faded into dawn, Jesus knelt in prayer.

It was there, early next morning, that his companions found him. From among them he called exactly twelve to be his close disciples, the inner circle of chosen friends. These twelve were Peter, with his brother Andrew; James and John, also brothers; Nathanael, sometimes called Bartholomew; Philip, Matthew, Thomas; James and Thaddaeus; Simon the Zealot (to distinguish him from Simon Peter); and Judas Iscariot.

Now that it was daylight these twelve all set off with Jesus, a happy company together. They walked steadily along the mountain, until they found a level place where they, and many others who had come to listen to Jesus, might sit while he taught them. Most of that day he sat on the gentle slope of the hillside, with the twelve at his feet and the silent crowds beyond them, hanging on his words.

And what words they were! He taught them about a new kingdom, God's Kingdom, the Kingdom of heaven. He taught them about loving enemies, about treasure in heaven, about secret prayer. He told them that no man can serve two masters; and that if a man sets himself to put God first, then God will look after him, just as he feeds the birds and clothes the wild flowers.

'Ask and it shall be given you,' Jesus told them. 'Always treat others as you would like them to treat you.' And last of all he told them that it was not enough just to come and *hear* his teaching: his followers must *live* by what he taught. Listen to how he brought the day's teaching to a close:

'Everyone who hears these words of mine and puts them into practice is like a sensible man who built his house on the rock. Down came the rain and up came the floods, while the winds blew and roared upon that house – and it did not fall because its foundations were on the rock.

'But everyone who hears these words of mine and does not follow them can be compared with a foolish man who built his house on the sand. Down came the rains and up came the floods, while the winds blew and battered that house until it collapsed and fell with a great crash.'

And with that story fresh in their minds, searching their hearts and asking themselves whether their lives were built on rock or sand, the crowds followed Jesus down from the hillside, with his twelve chosen friends.

From Matthew's Gospel, chapter 5, Luke's Gospel, chapter 6

Dinner with Simon

'**M**aster,' said the Pharisee to Jesus, at the end of their talk together, 'will you not come home with me to dinner? I have some friends who would like to meet you.'

So Jesus walked home with the Pharisee, whose name was Simon, and was shown to a place at the low dinner table among the other guests. They all lay on couches, their feet away towards the wall, with one elbow resting on the table. They were all men: it was not the custom for women to share in dinner parties.

The meal began. Simon's friends had heard of Jesus and had many questions to ask. In the lamplit room a servant moved silently to and fro, filling the cups and carrying dishes. Suddenly the talk ceased: Simon raised his head and stared. All eyes turned to the open doorway, where a woman was standing.

They recognized her at once. To Simon and his friends she was well known as a woman with a bad reputation in the city. It was unthinkable that she should dare to

come to the house of a respectable Pharisee. Jesus knew her too. Only a day or two before she had listened to him teaching about the love of God for those who go astray; and he knew that, bad though her past life had been, she had found God's free forgiveness. She had come tonight to Simon's house simply to find Jesus again. She had a present for him.

While the servants waited not knowing what to do, and Simon frowned and the guests stared, the woman came forward into the room and stood by Jesus' couch. She was weeping softly, and as her tears fell on his feet, she wiped them with the tresses of her hair. Perhaps it was sorrow for the past that made her weep; or joy for her new-found forgiveness. But whether in joy or sorrow, her tears were tears of love. Then she brought out from her dress a little alabaster bottle of perfume – perhaps the most precious of her treasures – and poured it gently over Jesus' feet.

At that, Simon broke silence. He was very put out to have such a woman behave like this at his dinner party.

'If this fellow were really a prophet,' he whispered loudly to his neighbour, pointing across at Jesus, 'he would know who this is that touches him. He would have realized that she is a bad woman.'

Jesus turned to him. 'Simon,' he said softly, 'there is something I want to say to you.'

'Very well, Master,' replied Simon. 'Say it.'

'Once upon a time,' said Jesus, 'there were two men in debt to the same moneylender. One owed him a great deal of money, the other a small amount. And since they were unable to pay, he let them both off. Now, which of them do you suppose will love him most?'

'Well,' said Simon, 'I should think the one that was let off the most.'

'Exactly,' replied Jesus. And he went on to remind Simon of what the woman had done for him, and how she had shown her love.

'I tell you,' said Jesus, 'her great love proves that her many sins have been forgiven; where little has been forgiven, little love is shown.' And then Jesus said to the woman, 'Your sins are forgiven.'

Simon and his friends looked at one another in dismay. 'Who *is* this man,' they began to ask themselves, 'that he can forgive sins?'

But Jesus turned to the woman as she was about to leave. 'Your faith has saved you,' he told her gently. 'Go in peace.'

From Luke's Gospel, chapter 7

33

Sowing Seeds

It had been cool indoors, but the streets of Capernaum were like an oven. Jesus made his way out of the house where he was staying and toward the lakeside. Under a cloudless sky the blue water of the Sea of Galilee sparkled in the early sunshine, and the fine white sand was hot to the feet.

Already a crowd had collected, and when they saw Jesus coming others ran to join them. Merchants and fishermen, old men hobbling over the beach, children and passers-by, they pushed and jostled one another, talking all the time, trying to get near the Master.

Down by the water's edge Peter had found an old friend, a fisherman back from his night's work, his fish sold and his boat cleaned, the thwarts and bottom-boards still shining wetly in the sun. Peter explained what he wanted, and then helped the fisherman to push the boat out into the clear shallows, the keel grating on the stones. Jesus climbed aboard – how cool the water after the burning sand – and after two quick strokes of an oar they dropped the anchor overboard with a splash, only a few yards from shore.

The crowd, who had thought at first that Jesus was slipping away from them, soon saw what was in his mind. One after another, they began to sit down contentedly on the shelving sand. Now that Jesus was in the boat, everyone could see and everyone could hear. A great silence settled on the beach, broken by the lapping of the small waves, and the voice of Jesus, clear and strong, telling one of his stories. Perhaps Jesus could see a farmer at work among the olive gardens and the vineyards on the hills above the lake. To and fro, to and fro, would go the farmer, sowing his seed. At any rate, here is the story Jesus told:

'There was once a man who went out to sow. And as he sowed, some seed fell along the footpath; and the birds came and gobbled it up. Some fell on stony patches where it had very little soil. It sprouted quickly in the shallow soil, but when the sun rose the young corn was scorched, and as it had no root it withered away. Some seed fell among thistles; and the thistles shot up, and choked the corn. And some of the seed fell into good soil and produced a good crop – some a hundred times what had been sown, some sixty and some thirty times.' And then Jesus added, 'The man who has ears to hear should use them!'

Jesus went on to tell the crowd on the beach some other stories; but later, when he was alone, the twelve disciples asked the meaning of his story about the sower, and the different kinds of soil. He explained that the four kinds of soil onto which the seed fell are like four different ways in which people listened to his teaching.

The seed on the footpath is like a

man who does not really understand. Satan, the evil one, quickly snatches away the word that was sown in his heart.

The seed on the stony and shallow ground is like a man who eagerly accepts the message; but he has a shallow heart. When trouble comes he gives up his faith at once.

The seed among thistles is like the man who hears Jesus' teaching and would be glad to follow it; but somehow he is always busy, with much to think about and many pleasures, and these are like fast-growing thistles that choke the seed. He finds no room for it in his overcrowded life.

'But the seed on good soil,' said Jesus to the twelve, 'is the man who both hears and understands the message. His life shows a good crop.'

And so the disciples began to understand also what Jesus meant by saying 'The man who has ears to hear should use them!' For in his story, it was always the same seed. What made the difference was the listening heart, ready and eager to understand and to obey.

From Mark's Gospel, chapter 4, Luke's Gospel, chapter 8

Storm on the Water

Peter was enjoying himself immensely. It had been a long day but a good one. Quite early in the morning Jesus had come to the lakeside to teach. All day Jesus had taught the people from a borrowed boat, anchored a few yards out in the shallow water, while the crowd sat on the shore. There are no tides on the Sea of Galilee, but Peter had found plenty to do. He had seen to the anchors, tending the ropes with every change of the wind. At midday he had found some food from one of his friends among the fishermen, and Jesus and the twelve had shared it together in the gently rocking boat. Now it was evening, and Peter was taking charge again.

Jesus had just finished preaching. He turned to Peter and the others and said, 'Let us cross over to the other side of the lake.' Peter was delighted. His friend, the boat's owner, was perfectly willing. The lake was only six miles across – they could still see the further shore quite clearly in the pale light of evening. But first, with

his brother Andrew and some of the others, Peter waded ashore to persuade the crowds that Jesus would not be teaching any more that day, and it was time to go home.

Presently the beach was empty. Peter and the others climbed aboard. The anchors were brought in and the patched sail hoisted. It flapped for a moment until the offshore breeze caught it, and they set off across the lake. Capernaum and its familiar beach grew smaller behind them as they made for open water through the gathering dark. Apart from a few other small boats nearby they were alone at last. Jesus, tired out after a full day's teaching, slept soundly on a leather cushion in the stern.

It grew darker and colder. The fishermen among the disciples were watching the clouds gathering, shutting out the first stars. They glanced uneasily at one another. Then a strong puff of wind brought with it a shower of spray. The waves were growing bigger. A storm was blowing up.

'Better have that sail down quick,' said one of the men. Two others jumped to the oars to keep the boat head to wind. They were none too soon. A violent squall, leaping down from the low-lying hills surrounding them, whipped up the water until the boat was tossing like a cork. A huge wave splashed inboard, soaking the disciples and filling the bottom of the boat. The wind, at gale force now, and frightening in the darkness, howled across the water. More waves crashed into the little boat until it was all but swamped. In the stern, tired out, Jesus slept on.

Two of the disciples, soaking wet and terrified, hurriedly shook him awake.

'Master,' they shouted above the noise of the wind, 'Master, don't you care that we are drowning?'

Jesus was awake at once. He looked at the frightened men in the sinking boat; and then at the clouds racing low over the night sky, and at the angry sea. Swaying with the motion of the boat, he got to his feet and spoke to the wind and the waves. His voice, to which the twelve had listened all that sunlit day, rang out anew across the dark water above the raging of the storm: 'Peace,' said Jesus to the wind and waves, 'Peace, be still!'

Even as he spoke, the wind dropped and there was a dead calm. The motion of the boat died away. The noise of the wind ceased. Jesus turned to his friends: 'Why are you so frightened?' he asked them. 'What has happened to your faith?'

But the disciples were filled with fear and wonder at what they had seen. As they set to work to put the boat in order, they kept saying to one another, 'Whoever can he be? – even the wind and the waves do what he tells them!'

From Mark's Gospel, chapter 4, Luke's Gospel, chapter 8

An Only Daughter

'There's quite a crowd on the beach,' said one of the twelve disciples, shading his eyes with his hand. 'I think it's us they're waiting for.'

The others followed his pointing finger. Sure enough, the beach at Capernaum, still a mile or two away across the water, was thronged with people.

Jesus and his friends were on their way back across the Sea of Galilee. They had sailed over in a night of storm; now they were returning in a day of bright sunshine. The boat rode happily on the gentle swell; the old sail filled nicely in the light breeze. Soon the keel grounded gently on the stones, and after splashing through the shallows, Jesus was again on dry land – and again surrounded by an excited crowd.

But the crowd soon parted to make way for a man who was clearly on urgent business. He was a well-known figure in the town. One of the bystanders nudged his friend and pointed: 'See him?' he said. 'That's Jairus, that tall fellow there, one of the rulers of the synagogue. What does he want with Jesus in such a hurry?' A ruler of the synagogue was an important man.

Jairus meanwhile had shouldered his way through to where Jesus was standing. He fell on his knees at Jesus' feet, saying: 'Master, my little girl is dying. I beg you to come and lay your hands on her to cure her and save her life.'

So Jesus went with him, and the crowd followed at their heels.

Now among the crowd was a sick woman. For twelve years she had gone from one doctor to another, but none of them had been able to make her better. She had heard about Jesus, and now she saw her chance. She came up behind him in the crowd, and touched his cloak. 'For if I can only touch his clothes,' she said to herself, 'I shall be cured.' So she touched him. And at once she knew that she was well.

But Jesus stopped. He knew that power had gone out of him. He turned to the crowd and said: 'Who touched my clothes?'

The disciples were puzzled by his question. 'You can see the crowd jostling you,' they said. 'How can you ask "Who touched me?"'

But Jesus scanned the faces following him; and soon the woman came forward, trembling and afraid, and fell at his feet and told him the whole story.

'Daughter,' Jesus said to her, 'it is your faith that has healed you – go in peace.'

Meanwhile, as Jesus still stood talking to the woman, Jairus saw one of his servants hurrying to speak with him. This was the tragic message: 'Your daughter is dead – there is no need to trouble the Master any further.'

It was a bitter blow. Jairus' daughter was an only child, just twelve years old, and the light of his life. All at once he looked old and sad.

But Jesus had heard the servant's message too. 'Don't be afraid,' he said to Jairus. 'Just go on believing.' Then he told the disciples to keep back the crowd, while with Peter and James and John they hurried on to Jairus' house.

The mourners were already there, weeping and wailing for the dead child. But Jesus took his companions, with Jairus and his wife, into the room where their daughter lay. Gently he lifted the small limp hand and spoke to her: 'Get up, my child.'

The pale eyelids flickered: the child stirred. Before their eyes she got to her feet, quite recovered, and walked across the room. Jesus told Jairus and his wife to give her some food; but to say nothing to anyone of what had happened. Then he and his friends slipped quietly away, leaving the two astonished parents overcome with joy.

From Luke's Gospel, chapter 8

Picnic in the Hills

To this day, nobody knows his name. He was just a boy who lived over the hills by the Sea of Galilee. One fine afternoon his mother sent him out with a picnic supper in his pocket, and told him to be sure and come home before dark.

On the hillside by the lake, to his great surprise, he found a crowd of people – more people than he had ever seen in his life before. There were farmers and peasants, women and children, babies and dogs, all sitting on the green grass in the late spring sunshine, listening to Jesus. As Jesus looked at them, he loved them and his heart went out to them. They were his fellow-countrymen. He told them how God loved them too.

By the time he had finished speaking, the sun was low in the sky, and it was growing cold. The twelve disciples urged Jesus to send the

people home. It was late, they said, and most of them were tired and hungry, and some had a long way to go. But because he loved them, Jesus said they must first have supper; then they should go home.

The puzzled disciples did not know what to do when they heard this. They had no food with them, and there was nowhere nearby where they could buy any. Only the boy from over the hills had his picnic supper – and he shyly offered that to Andrew if it was any help. And so as not to disappoint him, Andrew told Jesus. There were five thousand hungry people waiting; and here were five little barley rolls and two small dried fish. Jesus looked at them, and looked at Andrew, and looked at the boy; and

then he told the disciples to make the crowd sit down again.

By now they had all begun to get up and stretch their legs and collect their children and start for home; but before long the disciples had them all sitting down again, in neat rows on the green hillside.

Jesus took the napkin with the five rolls and the two dried fish, and looked up to heaven and said a prayer, thanking God for the food. And then he began to break the food up with his fingers, and give it in handfuls to the twelve disciples, for them to carry it to the crowd. Handful after handful after handful – and still there was more.

In the end, there was enough for everyone – and a lot left over if anyone had wanted more. Happy and fed and satisfied, the people drifted home. The boy, too, full of fish and barley bread, walked slowly home in the twilight, his mind busy with what he had heard and seen. Perhaps, too, he was thinking to himself that if you give even a very little into the hands of Jesus, there is no knowing what he can do with it.

From Luke's Gospel, chapter 9, John's Gospel, chapter 6

Night on the Lake

One by one the lights went out in the houses along the shore. By this time everyone was in bed, wrapping the blankets close about them while the wind rattled the shutters. But Jesus and his friends were still out of doors, a little chilly in the night air, and a long way from home.

After the crowd of the afternoon had been given supper (a picnic supper, you remember) and had gone away, Jesus climbed to the top of a hill by the Sea of Galilee to pray to his Father alone and undisturbed. He told his twelve disciples to take the boat across to the far side of the Sea (which is really a big inland lake) and wait for him to join them.

By the light of the full moon, Peter and the other fishermen soon found the boat pulled up on the beach. They were used to boats, and helped their friends aboard, pushing off from the shore. Then, taking an oar each, they settled down to row.

Once away from the shelter of the land the wind blew more strongly, dead against them. Soon the boat was pitching and rolling on a choppy sea, the bare mast jolting against the stars. Some of the twelve began to feel sea-sick. They were all cold and wet with the wind and spray. The lake seemed very wide, the waves bigger with every moment, the boat very small and Jesus far away.

Suddenly the moon shone through a gap in the racing clouds. Behind them, halfway between the boat and the blackness of the land, the figure of a man appeared, walking on the sea. Huddled together in the rocking boat the disciples cried out in fear.

'It is a ghost!' said one of them.

The voice of Jesus came to them above the wind: 'It is I. Don't be afraid.'

'Lord, if it is really you,' said Peter, 'tell me to come to you on the water.'

Jesus said to him, 'Come.'

Watched by the others, Peter put first one foot and then the other over the side of the tossing boat. He let go with his hands, and began to walk across the water to go to Jesus. The wind tugged at his coat; beneath his feet there were only the waves, black and hungry under the moon. He looked down: his courage failed him and he began to sink.

'Lord, save me,' cried Peter. And Jesus was there at once beside him. He reached out a hand and caught him, and together they climbed aboard. As they did so, the wind dropped; the violence of the waves died away; all was well. The twelve disciples looked at one another and then at Jesus.

'Ship your oars,' called the helmsman. They found themselves gliding through the shallows towards the farther beach. The fears of the night were over. It seemed like a dream, that Jesus had walked to join them across the water. But in their hearts they knew that it was true, and wondered what it might mean.

From Matthew's Gospel, chapter 14

'Who do you say I am?'

It was hot work trudging through the sunshine. Andrew stopped for a minute to straighten his back and rest. Jesus and his twelve disciples were walking steadily northwards from Galilee on the Roman road towards Mount Hermon. Every time they lifted their eyes the mountain was there ahead of them, its snow-capped peaks growing loftier and larger with every mile.

Another hour, and Jesus called a halt. They all sat down together in the shade of a rock by the wayside for a picnic lunch. They dipped their hot hands and faces in a nearby stream, still ice-cold from the mountain springs.

After lunch Jesus wandered a little away from the others, who were chatting among themselves, to find a quiet place where he could pray undisturbed to his heavenly Father. Presently, when he came back to

where his friends were resting, he said he had a question for them.

'Who do people say I am?' he asked them.

The disciples looked at one another. They heard a great deal of talk on this subject among the villagers and bystanders, wherever Jesus was. There had been all kinds of wild stories going the rounds in Galilee.

'Some people are saying you are John the Baptist,' said one of the twelve.

'Or Elijah,' said another.

'Yes,' they agreed. 'John the Baptist, or Elijah, or one of the prophets, come back to life again.'

Jesus nodded. It was very much the answer he had expected. Now he had another question for them: what did *they* think of him, these twelve friends and disciples? For the first time he put to them the direct question: 'Who do *you* say that I am?'

No one said anything for a moment. They knew him so well. They had lived with him for a long time now, sharing food and shelter, sailing boats and sleeping rough, talking long into the night by small-burning campfires under Galilean stars. But who *was* he – this Jesus? All at once they were shy of him. No one wanted to be the first to speak.

Except Peter. Peter would always be ready to plunge in. 'You? You are Christ,' he said, the words tumbling over themselves in his excitement, 'the Son of the living God.'

And even as Peter said it, he knew it was the truth. This Jesus, whom they knew so well, was the Son of God, come down to live as a man among them, to teach them, love them, heal them, and save them from their sins. It was a great moment for Peter, and one he would always remember . . .

'Who do you say I am?' Jesus had asked them; and he, Peter, had found the answer: 'You are Christ, the Son of the living God.'

From Luke's Gospel, chapter 9

The Voice of God

Peter's legs were aching and the flies were troubling him. He stopped climbing for a moment and looked back. There, not far below him on the hillside, was Jesus climbing steadily. James and John panted upwards a little way behind. It was warm work. Away below them stretched the bare landscape, green and brown, still and lifeless as far as the eye could see. Above them – a long way above them, thought Peter, shading his eyes – towered the summit.

Presently Jesus stopped climbing and they lay full-length on the soft turf, resting in a companionable silence, gazing up into the empty sky. Peter's eyes soon closed; and in a moment the three disciples were fast asleep.

But Jesus was not sleeping. He had come to this deserted hillside to be quiet and to talk to his heavenly Father. His mind was full of what lay ahead of him, because soon now they must start southwards for Jerusalem; and there the religious leaders would oppose him and reject him. He knew that to go to Jerusalem was to go to pain and suffering and death. No wonder, while the disciples lay sleeping on the hillside, that Jesus prayed.

Had the disciples been watching, they would have noticed after a while that his face was changing. A trick of the light, they might have thought; but it was more than that. His whole face began to glow with the radiance of heaven: his very clothes became

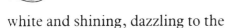

white and shining, dazzling to the eyes.

And suddenly he was not alone. Two other shining figures, their bearded faces full of light and joy, stood there on the hillside deep in serious talk with Jesus. One was Moses, to whom long ago the Law of God was given; and the other Elijah, one of God's faithful prophets. They had lived on earth hundreds of years before; and now for a short time they had returned in glory from the world beyond to talk with Jesus about what was soon to happen at Jerusalem.

Perhaps it was the murmur of their talk that woke the sleeping disciples. James and John rubbed their eyes, gazing at Jesus seen for a moment in his true glory. As they sat there drinking in the scene, Peter burst into speech:

'Master,' he said, 'it is wonderful for us to be here. Let us put up three shelters of leafy branches – one for you, one for Moses, and one for Elijah.' He was so excited he hardly knew what he was saying! And before he finished speaking the air grew suddenly colder, and a cloud from the hilltop wrapped itself about them like a mist: and from the cloud a voice spoke, saying, 'This is my Son, my chosen. Listen to him.'

The disciples fell on their faces in fear and reverence at the voice of God. Presently a hand touched them, and they looked up into the face of Jesus. The cloud had passed, and the shining glory; Moses and Elijah had returned to heaven. The Jesus they had seen for a moment in his true likeness, as the Lord of Glory and the King of Kings, they saw now once more – for a little longer – as the friend they loved and knew and followed: who was yet the chosen Son of God.

From Luke's Gospel, chapter 9

A Man born Blind

One Sabbath day, Jesus and his friends had been to the Temple. On their way out they passed a young man, quite blind, sitting by the Temple gate. It was well known in Jerusalem that he had been born blind, and had never known what it was to see.

As they walked past, one of Jesus' twelve disciples asked him why this poor man had been born blind – was it in some way his own fault? Or was it because his parents had done wrong, and this was the result?

'He was not born blind because of his own sin or that of his parents,' Jesus told them, 'but to show the power of God at work in him. While I am in the world, I am the light of the world.'

As he said this, Jesus stopped beside the blind man and bent down. He spat on the dusty ground and made clay with his fingers, and gently smeared it on the young man's poor blind eyes.

'Now,' Jesus said to him, 'go and wash in the pool of Siloam' – a spring with steps down to the water, just nearby. The blind man did as Jesus told him. He felt his way down the steps, and splashed the cool water on his face to wash away the clay; and as he did so, he discovered he could *see*.

Of course when he went home, his friends could hardly believe it. They hurried out of their houses to look at him, and gathered together whispering excitedly.

'Isn't this the blind man who used to sit and beg?' they asked one another.

'It's very like him,' they agreed.

But they could hardly believe it really was the same man – blind all his life, and now seeing as well as any of them. But the man himself soon told them all about it.

'The man called Jesus made some clay,' he said, 'and smeared it on my eyes; and then he said "Go to Siloam and wash". So I went and washed – and that's how I got my sight.'

His friends took the man to see the Pharisees, the religious leaders of the city, who had no love for Jesus. At first they would not believe the story at all. They sent for the man's parents and questioned them closely. But his parents told them that he had been born a blind baby, and had not been able to see all his life long until that day. When the Pharisees heard that, and knew there was no denying it,

they became very angry, saying that it was quite wrong that Jesus should have healed the man on the Sabbath day, when it was against the law to work. They even tried to say that Jesus could not be a good man if he did not respect their Sabbath, but the blind man interrupted them.

'One thing I am sure of,' he said. 'I used to be blind; now I can see. If this man had not come from God, he couldn't do such a thing.'

And in their hearts, most of Jerusalem agreed with him.

From John's Gospel, chapter 9

The Good Shepherd

It was wintertime in Jerusalem, and Jesus was often in the Temple teaching. The Pharisees were not at all pleased to find so many people always ready to gather around Jesus and listen to him. Some of them even said he was doing the devil's work.

But others thought deeply about his wise teaching, and remembered the man born blind, and said, 'No one possessed by an evil spirit could speak like this. Could an evil spirit open blind men's eyes?'

What made some of them especially angry was to hear Jesus telling the people about himself. In their Bible, which is our Old Testament, they often read about God their Father as a Shepherd of his people, and about themselves as God's flock of sheep. But now Jesus was saying, '*I* am the good shepherd.' Listen to his words:

'I am the good shepherd; the good shepherd will give his life for the sake of the sheep. But the hired man who is not the shepherd and does not own the sheep, will see the wolf coming, desert the sheep and run away. And the wolf will attack the flock and send them flying. The hired man runs away because he is only a hired man and has no interest in the sheep. I am the good shepherd and I know those that are mine, and my sheep know me, just as the Father knows me and I know the Father. And I am giving my life for the sake of the sheep.

'And I have other sheep who do not belong to this fold, whom I must bring in and they too will hear my voice. So there will be one flock and one shepherd. This is the reason why the Father loves me – that I lay down my life, and I lay it down to take it up again. No one is taking it from me.' (Jesus looked at the Pharisees as he said this, for he knew they hated him in their hearts and would be glad to see him killed.) 'No one is taking it from me, but I lay it down of my own

free will. I have the power to lay it down and I have the power to take it again. This charge I have received from my Father.'

This is what Jesus said to those who came to him in the Temple to hear his teaching. In this way, talking of sheep and shepherds, he told them (if they had been able to understand) of how he would die to save sinners and rise again from the dead.

'My sheep,' Jesus told them, 'my sheep hear my voice and I know who they are. They follow me and I give them eternal life. They will never die and no one shall snatch them from my care.'

From John's Gospel, chapter 10

'The Man who was hurt by Robbers

One day Jesus was talking with a man who loved an argument. The man was a lawyer, and he had been quoting the Jewish law which said that you must love God with all your heart; and love other people as yourself.

'But what does that mean?' said this man to Jesus.

He hoped, maybe, that Jesus would tell him that the law meant he should love his friends, or the people of his village, or even all his fellow-Jews.

By way of answer, Jesus began to tell a story. The people standing around smiled at one another, and drew a little closer so that they would not miss anything. They loved a story as much as anyone.

Jesus' story was about a man on a journey. He was walking from Jerusalem to the city of Jericho nearly twenty miles away. It was well known as a dangerous road, twisting and turning among desolate and rugged hills which were the homes of thieves and bandits. As soon as Jesus spoke of the Jerusalem-to-Jericho road most of his hearers guessed that someone journeying alone might be attacked and robbed.

And this is just what happened. On a deserted stretch of road, with no help in sight, a band of robbers sprang out of hiding. The man put up a fight, but they were too many for him. In a few minutes it was all over. They stole his money and his luggage and most of his clothes and vanished into the hills. Bruised and bleeding, the man lay half-dead by the side of the road. Unless someone came to help him soon, he was sure to die.

The dust settled; the sun beat down; all was silence on the Jerusalem-to-Jericho road.

Then in the distance came the sound of footsteps. Round the bend in the road there appeared another man on a journey – a priest returning to Jerusalem. How lucky that he should have come by just now! The priest caught sight of the poor still body by the edge of the road, and he was afraid. There would be robbers not far away. Perhaps they were even now in hiding, waiting for their next victim.

'Poor man,' thought the priest to himself. 'I wish I could stop to help him.' But he hurried by on the other side of the road.

The minutes passed. Someone else came in sight, one of the Temple officials from Jerusalem, a respected and religious man. But like the priest, he only quickened his step, and tried not to look at the body of the wounded man as he hurried past on the other side.

Then, in the distance, clip-clopping along on a donkey, came yet a third man. He came from Samaria, a Samaritan. Now, the Jews hated Samaritans as enemies and foreigners. But this man stopped his donkey, and went to help the wounded man. He bandaged his cuts and bruises, lifted him on to the back of the donkey, and set off to find an inn.

All that night the Samaritan nursed the wounded man, and in the morning he paid the bill for both of them, and promised the innkeeper money if he would care for him until he was well again.

Jesus' hearers did not enjoy that story much. They shuffled their feet and looked at the ground. They disliked the Samaritans, and did not want to hear of one so brave and generous and kind. But when Jesus asked them, 'Which of these three showed love to the man who fell among the robbers?' they could only agree that it was the foreigner from Samaria.

Jesus looked around at their sullen faces and said simply, 'Go and do as he did.'

From Luke's Gospel, chapter 10

Martha and Mary

Martha's garden was cool and full of green shade. After the heat and dust of the journey it was wonderful to sit and rest under the leafy branches. Jesus thankfully eased his weary legs into the most comfortable position, and relaxed. This was Bethany, a village on the road. A mile or two away beyond the garden were the slopes of the Mount of Olives, and beyond them the city of Jerusalem. But that was tomorrow's journey; tonight it was enough to be Martha's guest at Bethany, and to sit in the peaceful garden and wait for supper.

Supper, it was plain, was going to be something special. Martha and her younger sister Mary had given him a wonderful welcome; and now from the house came the sounds of preparation. Enticing smells, full of herbs and spices, wafted across the evening air.

Martha was determined to serve the best supper she could for her very special guest. She had set out the meal under the fig tree, and every moment saw her scurrying backwards and forwards, talking busily to herself under her breath: 'I wonder if there will be enough cheese and olives – I'll just run and get some more . . . I know there's something I've forgotten . . .' and she would gaze for a moment at the laden table, lost in thought, until a hiss of steam told her that a pot was boiling over on the hot fire.

Mary, meanwhile, was entertaining their guest. She had come out from the house a little while before to see that Jesus was comfortable, and had everything he wanted, as he rested before the meal. Like her sister, Mary had been looking forward very much to seeing Jesus again, and there was a lot to talk about. She settled down at his feet, talking, questioning and listening to all that he had to say.

At last Martha could stand it no longer. She came suddenly over to where Jesus was sitting and, going rather red in the face, she burst out: 'Lord, don't you *care* that my sister has left me to do everything by myself? Tell her to get up and help me.'

Mary started to say something, but Jesus answered for her. His voice was gentleness itself. He loved them both.

'Martha, my dear,' he said, 'you are fretting and fussing about so many things; but only a few things are really needed, perhaps only one. Mary has chosen the better part, and you must not take it away from her.'

Martha must often have thought of what Jesus said to her that evening. He was not ungrateful for all she was doing; but she needed to be reminded that people matter more than meals. And when next Jesus came to Bethany, it was Martha who was the first to go out to meet him.

From Luke's Gospel, chapter 10

Jesus Prays

It was a quiet and sleepy place. The twelve disciples watched Jesus wander off by himself, a little way apart from where they were sitting and talking together, and kneel down on the grass in the shadow of a rock to pray.

No one said anything: the murmur of conversation died away. They were twelve men left alone with their thoughts. The silence deepened until they could hear the insects buzzing among the branches overhead; in the distance a bird was calling; a long way off there was the murmur of a stream. Some slept peacefully, nodding in the sunshine. But at least one of the twelve disciples was doing some hard thinking.

'The Master's praying again,' he thought to himself. 'We've seen it so many times, we think nothing of it any longer. It's just something he does often, and we don't very much. I wonder what he *says* to his Father in heaven, how exactly they talk together, day after day. Sometimes it's only for a minute or two, sometimes for hours on end. I wish *I* knew how to pray.'

The wakeful disciple cast his mind back over some of the months he had spent in Jesus' company. There was that time – Capernaum, wasn't it? – when Jesus had preached in the synagogue, quite early on in their days together. By evening, the whole city had gathered outside the house where he was staying, hundreds of them blocking the road. He had been healing and helping anxious people far into the night. They had all been exhausted by the time they had got to bed. And the next morning when they woke up, Jesus was missing. Peter had found him at last, soon after dawn, all by himself, kneeling in prayer.

And that other time too (the disciple remembered), when Jesus had made the twelve of them set off by boat across the Sea of Galilee to Bethsaida, while he had gone alone into the hills – to pray. Oh, and there had been many, many such times.

But now Jesus had finished his prayer and was coming back to join them. The wakeful disciple scrambled to his feet, and went to meet Jesus. He had a request to make. 'Lord,' he said, 'teach us to pray, as John taught his disciples.'

The others had woken up by this time, rubbing their eyes and blinking in the sunlight. Jesus looked around at their twelve friendly and familiar faces, and this was his reply: 'When you pray, say

Our Father
May your name be honoured –
May your kingdom come!
Give us each day our daily bread
And forgive our sins
As we too forgive all those who
    have done us wrong.
And lead us not into temptation
But deliver us from evil.'

This, the Lord's own prayer, is the only one we know of that Jesus ever taught his friends. Across the world, in every age and language, the friends of Jesus have used it ever since.

From Luke's Gospel, chapter 11

27

Joy in Heaven

'Really, it's quite disgraceful,' the tall Pharisee was thinking to himself.

He was one of the most respected religious leaders among his own circle of friends – an influential man in city affairs. Just now he was standing listening to Jesus, among a crowd of passers-by. It was these passers-by who were worrying him.

'Bad characters, some of them,' he thought to himself. 'I can't see what there is about this man Jesus that makes these people want to come and listen to him. Half of them are up to no good, I'll be bound. Those three over there are tax-collectors; and I can't say I like the look of any of their friends. If we're not careful, this man Jesus will be giving religion a bad name among respectable people.'

The tall Pharisee shifted his weight from one foot to the other – it was very tiring, standing about and listening at street corners – and at that moment the person next to him, another of the religious leaders, leaned across to murmur something in his ear. He spoke in a low confidential whisper.

'This fellow,' he said – nodding his head to where Jesus was standing – 'This fellow welcomes sinners and even eats with them.'

The thought of sitting down to a meal with anyone less highly respectable than themselves filled the Pharisees with horror; yet it was well known that Jesus often had his meals as the guest of the strangest people – families who never came near the Temple, and had little or no respect for the Pharisees, and a bad reputation with the authorities.

It was a constant grumble of the Pharisees that Jesus, who claimed to be a religious teacher, was not more careful of the company he kept. He not only went to homes where they would never dream of setting foot; but he was made welcome, and counted some of these bad characters as *friends*!

It was perfectly true what was being whispered to the Pharisee on the edge of the crowd: 'This fellow welcomes sinners (think of it! *sinners*!) and even eats with them.'

But Jesus knew what they were saying about him. And instead of protesting or arguing, he told this story:

'If anyone owned a hundred sheep, and lost one of them, wouldn't he leave the ninety-nine to themselves in the open, and go after the one which is lost until he finds it?

And when he found it, he would put it on his shoulders with great joy, and as soon as he got home, he would call his friends together and say, "Come and celebrate with me, for I have found that sheep of mine which was lost."'

And Jesus went on to tell them that heaven itself rejoices more over one sinner who turns back to God than over many who belong to him already.

'In the same way, I tell you,' he said to them, 'there will be greater joy in heaven over one sinner who repents than over ninety-nine righteous people who have no need of repentance.'

From Luke's Gospel, chapter 15

28

The Younger Son

It was a very loud whisper. It reached the ears of Jesus as he was deep in talk with a little crowd of workmen, and one or two of the despised tax-collectors in the poorer quarter of the town.

'That fellow Jesus,' – the words could be heard quite plainly – 'That fellow Jesus ought to be more careful how he chooses his friends. There are some downright bad characters in that lot.'

This loud whisper was part of a conversation between two Pharisees standing together across the street and looking on with disapproval. The Pharisees were religious and respectable men, who found Jesus and his love for very ordinary people – even the mean and dishonest ones – hard to understand. So, to answer him, Jesus told this story.

'There was once a man who had two sons. The younger one said to his father, "Father, give me my share of the property". So he divided up his estate between the two of them. A few days later the younger son turned the whole of his share into cash and left home for a distant country, where he squandered it in reckless living.'

The Pharisees across the street looked even more disapproving. This was no way for a dutiful son to behave, spending all his father's money on pleasing himself and having a good time. But like everyone else they waited eagerly to hear what would happen next.

'When this younger son had run through all his money,' Jesus went on, 'a terrible famine fell upon that country, and he began to be in want. So he hired himself out to one of the local landowners who sent him into the fields to feed the pigs. He was so

hungry he would gladly have shared the food the pigs were eating; but no one gave him anything at all.

'Then he came to his senses and said, "To think of all my father's paid servants, with more food than they can eat, and here am I dying of hunger! I will start out and go back to my father, and I will say to him: 'Father, I have sinned against God and against you; I don't deserve to be called your son any more; please take me on as one of your paid servants'."'

In the little crowd gathered round Jesus, not a soul moved or spoke. They were thinking of this young man, son of a rich farmer, and what a mess he had made of things. To leave home as a son, and come back as a servant – what a come-down that would be! They hung on Jesus' words, waiting to hear whether the father would give the boy a job; or perhaps refuse to have him back at all.

'So he set out for his father's house,' Jesus continued, 'but while he was still a long way off, his father saw him and his heart went out to him. He ran to meet him, put his arms round him, and kissed him. The son said: "Father, I have sinned against God and against you; I don't deserve to be called your son any more." But the father said to his servants, "Quick! Fetch a robe, my best one, and put it on him; put a ring on his finger and shoes on his feet. Bring the fatted calf and kill it, and we will have a feast and a celebration! For this son of mine was dead and has come back to life. I thought I had lost him, and he's found!" And so the festivities began.'

Almost everyone who was listening to Jesus must have seen that this was a story about God. We are all like the boy who went away to the far country. How glad our heavenly Father is when we turn and come home.

From Luke's Gospel, chapter 15

29

To Wake the Dead

For the tenth time that day, Martha went to the door. Shading her eyes with her hand, she gazed into the distance along the road that led eastwards to the river. But there was no one to be seen. She sighed sadly and went indoors.

Inside the little house her sister Mary sat by the bedside of their brother Lazarus. For days now he had been very ill. Today he seemed much worse. The sisters had sent a message to Jesus, who was their friend, telling him about Lazarus; and as Mary looked at Martha she asked for the hundredth time the question that was in all their minds: 'Is Jesus coming? Is there any sign of him?' Martha shook her head.

That night, Lazarus died. They buried him in a cave in the hillside just beyond the village. Martha and Mary were desolate with grief and could hardly be comforted. And then, four days later, news reached them that Jesus was on his way.

Martha hurried out to meet him. 'If only you had been here, Lord,' she said to him, 'my brother would never have died.'

Jesus looked at her steadily: dear, kind Martha, her eyes full of tears. 'Your brother will rise again,' he said. 'The man who believes in me will live even though he dies. Can you believe that?'

'Yes, Lord,' said Martha. 'I do believe.'

Meanwhile Mary, too, set off to meet Jesus, and with the friends who had come to keep them company in their sorrow they all went to see the grave. The cave in the hillside where Lazarus was buried was closed by a great round stone.

Jesus wept as he stood there with Martha and Mary, and the people watching said to one another, 'Look how much he loved him.'

Suddenly Jesus said to them, 'Take away the stone.'

There was a shocked pause. Lazarus was dead and should be left in peace. Martha began to protest, but Jesus looked at her and she fell silent.

'Did I not tell you,' he said, 'that if you believed you would see the wonder of what God can do!' So in the end, rather scared and silent, they did what he wanted. They rolled the stone away from the dark mouth of the cave.

Then Jesus looked up to heaven and said, 'Father, I thank you that you have heard me, and I know that you always hear me.' When he had prayed he turned towards the open cave and called out loudly and clearly, 'Lazarus, come out.'

In absolute silence the people watched. Nothing stirred. A long minute passed. The tension grew. Then from the cave, like a man walking in his sleep, still bound in grave-clothes came Lazarus alive. He was well again, and warm and living; life had flooded back at the voice of Jesus. This was no dead man any longer; this was their brother Lazarus given back to them. Martha and Mary wept for joy.

The little crowd of villagers who had seen what happened hardly knew what to believe. They looked from Jesus to the cave, and from the cave to Lazarus, walking and talking, very much alive. Some of them became true followers of Jesus; but others, even with Lazarus alive among them, still would not believe.

From John's Gospel, chapter 11

30

The Children's Friend

The village street that morning seemed to be all children. It was still early, but the little group of women – the mothers of all these youngsters – had already been waiting for some time. They talked excitedly among themselves, one eye on the dark doorway across the street, and the other on small sons and daughters playing together in the dust at their feet. One or two of the women carried tiny babies wrapped in shawls, their brown eyes blinking in the sun.

Suddenly there was a stir of movement in the doorway opposite. Two of the leading men of the village emerged, followed by three or four of Jesus' disciples. Then came the moment for which the women had been waiting: Jesus himself appeared in the doorway, still deep in talk with one of his visitors.

The women looked at one another, collected their children about them, and began to move together across the street to where Jesus was standing. One of them, bolder than the rest, pressed forward to push her baby right against Jesus, trying to attract his attention. She knew – they all knew – that Jesus and his friends would be moving on soon toward another village. This would be their last opportunity to secure his blessing, not just for themselves but for their children, before he went on his way. It was for this they had gathered and waited. It was for this they pressed about him now.

But to see their Master, fresh from deep conversation with the most important men of the village, now hemmed in by a crowd of women and children was altogether too much for the disciples. They began to clear a way through the crowd, saying things like: 'Can't you see the Master's busy? He's late already, with a day's journey ahead of us. Move back now, please; clear the way; please stand back.'

By this time Jesus had finished saying goodbye to his visitors. Turning around, he saw at once what was happening, and the

disappointment on the faces of the women. He bent down, and picked up one of the children the disciples were trying to hold back.

'Never stop them,' said Jesus to the twelve. 'Let the little children come to me. The Kingdom of God belongs to such as these.'

Reluctantly the disciples drew back, now that they understood what Jesus wanted. The children began to cluster around him; and as he talked with them, so the other women held out their babies for him to touch and bless them. In a moment, Jesus looked up over the heads of the children to where the women were standing.

'I tell you,' he said to them, 'that whoever does not accept the Kingdom of God like a little child will never get into it at all.'

And with that he smiled at the little boy he was holding, put him gently down, and set off with his disciples on the road to the next village.

From Mark's Gospel, chapter 10, Luke's Gospel, chapter 18

31

The Man in the Tree

'If only,' Zacchaeus thought to himself, 'if only I was a few inches taller.'

He scuttled about at the back of the crowd, standing on tiptoe here, and trying to squeeze a way forward there, but it was no use. Whatever he tried, the people prevented him. Sometimes, he knew very well, they did it on purpose to spite him. 'Now then,' they said. 'No pushing there – we were here first.'

Poor Zacchaeus! He very much *wanted* to see Jesus, who was coming that way at any moment; but because he was such a short little man, all he actually *managed* to see were the broad backs of the men who lined the road in front of him.

At last, quite defeated, he stood for a moment in the shade of a fig-tree and mopped his brow. The tree had a great broad trunk, and low spreading branches – some of them stretching out over the heads of the crowd, and even across the road. It didn't look a hard tree to climb . . . And that is just what Zacchaeus did.

In a moment he had scrambled up the trunk, and was crawling out on one of the overhanging branches, shaded by the cool leaves. *Now* he could see the road; and in the distance where the dust was rising and the people running, Jesus himself was coming this way.

And so Zacchaeus waited. Down below, one or two of the men looked up at him and nudged one another

and whispered together. Zacchaeus knew they were making fun of him. He was a chief tax-collector and very rich. In those days people thought of tax-collectors as enemies and traitors because they collected taxes for the Romans. It was a sad and lonely face, hungry for friendship, that peered down between the green leaves of the fig-tree.

Zacchaeus watched closely as Jesus drew nearer. This was the man, he thought, whom they called 'Friend of tax-collectors'. He looked like a good friend to have . . . Just at that moment, Jesus stopped beneath the fig-tree and looked up.

'Zacchaeus,' called Jesus ('He knows my name,' thought Zacchaeus nearly falling out of his tree with excitement and surprise). 'Zacchaeus, hurry up and come down. You must be my host today.'

Zacchaeus wasted no time. He slid down the tree, his face beaming, bowed low before Jesus and the disciples, and led them to his house nearby. At the doorway he clapped his hands for the servants, ordering one to bring water to wash their feet, others to prepare a feast, others still to run to the market – 'fish, spices, lemons, fresh figs – the best they have'.

Some of the crowd had followed Jesus and stood by the doorway, muttering among themselves. 'Now this Jesus has gone to stay with a *real* sinner,' they said. Zacchaeus heard them, but he did not mind. He had come to a cross-roads. Having met Jesus, he could not go back to his old life of cheating and fraud.

Zacchaeus made his decision, and told Jesus: 'Look, Master,' he said 'I am going to give half my goods to the poor; and if I have swindled anybody out of anything, I will pay him back four times over.'

Everyone who heard this was astonished. The servants nearly dropped the dishes in surprise. Nobody had ever known Zacchaeus to give anything away before.

But to Jesus, it might have been the most natural thing in the world. 'Today salvation has come to this house,' he said to Zacchaeus, 'and this man too is a Son of Abraham.' He meant that Zacchaeus had shown himself no longer an outcast and a traitor, but one of the chosen people of God.

And to make it plain why he had wanted to stay with this little tax-collector, now beginning a new life, and not with one of the great or religious people of Jericho, Jesus added this: 'It was the lost that the Son of man came to seek and to save.'

From Luke's Gospel, chapter 19

32

Blind Bartimaeus

Bartimaeus lived in a beautiful city, Jericho 'the City of Palms', famous for its trees, its flowers and roses. Bartimaeus could smell the scent of the balsam groves and the heavy perfume of the summer flowers, but he could never see them. For Bartimaeus was blind.

Every morning, tap-tapping with his stick on the ground, Bartimaeus made his way through the city to sit with other blind men by the side of the road, to beg his living from the passers-by. The beggars' world was the sound of passing feet, voices and snatches of talk, dust and smells.

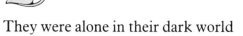

They were alone in their dark world though the sun shone ever more fiercely on their faces as the hours passed.

There was a stir in the city that morning. The sharp ears of blind Bartimaeus had already heard last night's news. Jesus the great prophet had come to Jericho with his disciples. There had been a large crowd out to meet him. And even now, as Bartimaeus listened, there was something different about the sounds from the city. In the distance still, but drawing nearer, were many feet, many voices; a crowd coming this way. From his seat by the roadside Bartimaeus enquired urgently of those nearby who had eyes to see.

'Who is it?' he asked them. 'What is happening? Tell a poor blind man.'

One of the bystanders looked back over his shoulder at the beggar. 'It is Jesus,' he said. 'That man they call Jesus of Nazareth is coming with his friends.'

When he heard that, Bartimaeus began to shout as loud as he could, to make Jesus hear before this chance was lost. 'Jesus,' he called, 'Jesus, Son of David, have pity on me.'

'Shut up,' said people in the crowd. 'Stop that noise, can't you?'

But Bartimaeus, and one of the other beggars with him, shouted and called even more loudly than before: 'Son of David, have pity on me.'

Suddenly Bartimaeus heard the footsteps come to a halt.

A voice above him said, not unkindly, 'Get up, he's calling you.'

Bartimaeus threw off his cloak and scrambled to his feet. Willing hands helped him forward into the road. The strong fingers of Jesus clasped his wrist. The crowd fell silent.

'What do you want me to do for you?' said the voice of Jesus. Bartimaeus knew just what he wanted.

'Oh Master, let me see again,' he said.

'Go your way,' said Jesus. 'Your faith has cured you.'

At those words, Bartimaeus felt the light coming back to his eyes. He put his hand to his face. Between his fingers, so bright he could hardly bear it, he *saw*. He saw the road, and the people around him, the yellow sunlight, the face of Jesus. Just as for others who had believed in him, so now for Bartimaeus this morning, Jesus had opened his eyes to a new world.

From Mark's Gospel, chapter 10, Luke's Gospel, chapter 18

33

The King Comes!

Two miles to go! Beyond the last grove of fig trees, just over the brow of the Mount of Olives, lay Jerusalem. Jesus and his friends, now that they were almost at the city, had spent an hour resting at the roadside before the last stage of their journey. They were silent in the midday sunshine, busy with their own thoughts. Presently Jesus spoke quietly to the two disciples beside him.

'Go into the village just ahead of you,' he said, pointing to a cluster of houses not far down the road. 'There you will find a colt tied – a colt no one has ever ridden. Untie it and bring it here to me. And if anybody asks you, "Why are you untying it?" just say "The Lord needs it".'

The two disciples set off; and at the entrance to the village, where two roads met, they found a house with two brown donkeys, mother and colt, tied to a ring in the wall. The donkeys stood patiently in the sunshine, swishing their tails to keep off the flies. At the sound of strangers the owner came to the doorway and asked 'Why are you untying that colt?'

'The Lord needs it,' said the disciples. The owner nodded, satisfied; and they led the donkeys, mother and colt together, back down the road to Jesus and the others. Two or three of them spread their cloaks to make a saddle on the colt's bony back, warm and dusty in the sun. Carefully Jesus mounted, firm hands gentle as

the colt trembled under him, and then the little company set off up the track toward Jerusalem.

A good many people had gathered by this time. Word had gone around that this was Jesus who had brought Lazarus back to life from that dark grave nearby. When they saw Jesus riding to Jerusalem, many remembered the old prophecy that this was how God's chosen King would come – not riding in state on a white charger; but meekly on a donkey, a young colt not fully grown.

Someone cheered, then someone else. Soon they were all cheering. They broke off the low branches from the palm trees to wave as flags, and to make a carpet of leaves on the road. Some even spread out their cloaks in the roadway, a patchwork for a royal progress.

From the top of the hill, Jerusalem lay spread out before them like a map; and when the donkey, picking its way delicately forward, began the descent to the city, the whole company began to sing and clap their hands in their excitement.

'God bless the King,' they cried. 'The King who comes in the name of the Lord! Peace in heaven and glory on high!'

So the children sang and danced before him: and the people clapped and shouted, and the palm branches waved and fluttered.

Only the Pharisees, watching with long faces at the street corners, grumbled and protested. 'The whole world has gone after him,' they muttered to one another. And one who could stand it no longer (for the Pharisees hated to see Jesus so popular) shouted across to him as the donkey passed by, 'Master, restrain your disciples.'

But Jesus said to him, 'I tell you that if they kept quiet, the very stones in the road would burst out cheering.'

And so they came to Jerusalem. Jesus wept to see the city which he loved, and where he was soon to die. He spent that night in Bethany with Martha and Mary; and the next morning he returned to Jerusalem and went to the Temple to teach. But he began, as he had begun once before on another visit, by driving out the traders in the Temple courts, overturning the tables of the moneychangers and the stallholders.

'It is written,' he told them, '"My house shall be a house of prayer" but you have made it a den of thieves.'

So day by day he taught in the Temple and the people hung upon his words.

From Matthew's Gospel, chapter 21, Luke's Gospel, chapter 19

34

Supper Together

'That's the man,' said Peter, clutching John's arm and pointing.

A servant was just coming around the corner toward them, carrying a pitcher of water. Jesus had instructed them to look for such a man and to follow him; so together the two disciples fell into step behind. The streets were crowded, but they saw him enter the curtained doorway of a house; and when Peter slipped in after him, it was to find that the owner of the house seemed to be expecting them.

Peter remembered the message Jesus had given them and said, 'The Master says "Where is the room where I and my disciples may eat the Passover?"' The Passover Supper was part of a very special festival, kept once a year by every Jewish family, in memory of how God had delivered his people long ago from captivity in Egypt.

The owner of the house beckoned to Peter and John, and led them by a flight of steps to an upper storey. He showed them a spacious room, furnished with couches and a low table; and on a dresser at the side stood cups and jugs, basins and dishes, all they were likely to need. And there, that same night, Jesus and his friends ate their last meal together.

When they had taken their places, propped up on the couches around the table, Jesus took a loaf, gave thanks to God, and broke it into pieces.

Then he passed it around, saying, 'This is my body which is given for you. Do this in remembrance of me.'

In the same way he passed around a cup of wine, saying, 'This is my blood of the covenant, shed for many. I tell you this: I will drink no more wine until the day comes when I drink it fresh in the Kingdom of God.'

When the cup had been passed from hand to hand in silence, Jesus rose from the table, fastened a towel about his waist, and poured water into a basin. Then, one by one, he began to wash the feet of the disciples.

'You call me "Master" and "Lord"' he said to them, 'and rightly so for that is what I am. Then if I, your Lord and Master, have washed your feet, you ought also to wash one another's feet. I have set you an example. You are to do as I have done for you.'

And then, much troubled, Jesus looked around at the twelve familiar faces, and told them that one of them was about to betray him to his enemies. By now it was nearly dark. Small lamps flickered on the tables, pools of brightness in the shadowed room.

The disciples looked at one another and began to ask, 'Is it I? Is it I?'

'Lord, who is it?' whispered John who was lying closest to Jesus on one of the couches.

'It is the man to whom I give this piece of bread when I have dipped it in the dish,' said Jesus. And with that, he dipped the bread in the dish before him and held it out to Judas Iscariot, saying, 'What you are going to do, do quickly.'

Some of them thought that Jesus was simply telling Judas to slip out to buy something (Judas looked after their money), or to do some other errand. Judas took the bread, rose from the table, and went out into the dark.

Alone together in the upper room, Jesus told the disciples (there were only eleven now) many things. He told them that, though he must go away, he would not leave them alone, but God's Holy Spirit would come to them. He told them not to be anxious. 'Set your troubled hearts at rest,' he said. 'Hold on to your faith in God and your faith in me. Keep my commandments. Peace is my parting gift to you.'

And then, his teaching done, he prayed to his Father for them all, that God would keep them faithful and united through the trouble coming, with his love strong in their hearts.

When Jesus had finished praying, they sang a hymn together for the last time. Then they blew out the lamps, closed the door behind them, and trooped in silence down the steps and out toward the dark hillside.

From Luke's Gospel, chapter 22, John's Gospel, chapter 13

35

Night in the Garden

In silence Jesus and the eleven disciples made their way toward the city gate. After the solemn words of Jesus in the upper room a few moments before, they were puzzled and beginning to be afraid. Things were happening that night which they did not understand.

They made their way past lighted windows where families still kept the feast, through a city humming with the sound of many voices. But these soon died away behind them as they passed through the great gate beyond the Temple. The moon was rising; but the valley of the river Kidron was dark below them, filled with the murmur of running water.

Presently they came to an enclosed garden – a garden called Gethsemane – full of gnarled old olive trees, shrubs and a few cypresses. In the moonlight it too was a place of shadows. Nothing stirred in the scented darkness.

Jesus himself, with Peter and James and John, left the other eight disciples resting near the entrance to Gethsemane, and pressed on among the trees to a clearing.

Jesus seemed different, more troubled than they had ever known him. 'My soul is nearly breaking,' he told the three of them. 'Stay here and keep watch with me.'

He plunged on further among the trees, and flung himself on the ground, to pray that if it were possible, he might be spared what lay ahead of him. 'Dear Father,' he said, 'all things are possible to you. Yet it is not what I want, but what you want.'

Soon he went back to where Peter and the others were waiting, and found them fast asleep. So again he fell on his face to the ground, repeating the same words in an agony of prayer. He came to them again, and still they were sleeping, so for the third time he prayed alone. When he came back at last, he spoke to them; and they started up, rubbing the sleep out of their eyes.

'Are you still sleeping?' he said. 'The moment has come. You are going to see the Son of Man betrayed into the hands of evil men. Look, here comes my betrayer!'

Even as he spoke, they heard not far away the sound of raised voices; and at the same time they caught the flash of lanterns and torches flickering among the trees. The men were coming closer; and as Peter and James and John stood motionless, Judas Iscariot slipped into the clearing. Behind him followed a crowd of armed men sent by the Chief Priests to arrest Jesus. Judas had known where to find him; and had led them to him. Here they could take Jesus prisoner secretly, away from the crowded streets, and free from the fear of any disturbance in the city.

When he had made his bargain with the Chief Priests, Judas had agreed upon a signal. 'The one I shall kiss is your man,' he told them. 'Seize him and get him safely away.' So now he stepped forward to where Jesus was standing, greeted him, and kissed him. And as he did so, the soldiers sprang forward upon Jesus, and held him fast. Then Jesus spoke:

'So you've come out with your swords and staves to capture me like a bandit, have you?' he asked. 'Day after day I was with you in the Temple, teaching, and you never laid a finger on me. But the scriptures must be fulfilled.'

The soldiers bound Jesus and led him away. One by one the disciples made their escape, slipping away through the trees to safety. One of his young followers was seized by the soldiers, but he slipped away from them, leaving his shirt in their hands, and took to his heels, panting through the trees in the moonlight, naked and afraid.

From Matthew's Gospel, chapter 26, Mark's Gospel, chapter 14, Luke's Gospel, chapter 22, John's Gospel, chapter 18

36

The House of Caiaphas

It was well past midnight by the time the soldiers had bound Jesus, and led him back over the brook toward Jerusalem. In the darkened street there was no other footfall, no light but their own lanterns and the moon. They came at last to the house of Caiaphas, to find lights burning and a company assembled.

Caiaphas was high priest; and when the soldiers had set out to arrest Jesus, he had sent messages to summon all the priests and religious leaders to a special council, so that Jesus might be put on trial there and then, at dead of night, without waiting until morning.

Peter and John had escaped the soldiers in the garden. They followed at a safe distance back into the city, and saw Jesus taken through a guarded doorway into the high priest's palace. Earlier that evening Peter had boasted that whatever the others might do, he would never let Jesus down.

'I am ready to go to prison or even to die with you,' he had declared.

Already he had forgotten Jesus' sad reply: 'I tell you, Peter, the cock will not crow tonight until you have three times denied that you know me.'

Now, through the doorway, Peter and John could see into the courtyard of the palace of Caiaphas. It was open to the sky, with a high gallery around it. Perhaps they caught a glimpse of a lighted window, or heard the mutter of voices as the priests accused Jesus, or questioned witnesses, or talked among themselves. John was known to some of the high priest's servants, and after a word to the woman who kept the gate, he and Peter were allowed in.

As they entered, the gatekeeper stared hard at Peter and said to him: 'Are you one of this man's disciples too?'

'No, I am not,' said Peter quickly, and passed on into the courtyard.

In the middle of the court a charcoal fire was burning, and a number of servants were gathered around it to keep warm. It was still only springtime, with a chill in the night air. Peter drifted over, as casually as he could, and stood among the servants, warming his hands. It was a brave thing to come like that to the very house where his Master was held prisoner.

Presently Peter noticed one of the maids eyeing him intently in the red glow from the fire. He stepped back into the shadows but it was too late.

'Surely you too are one of his disciples, aren't you?' said the maid.

Peter shook his head and denied it at once. 'No, I am not,' he said roughly and began to move away.

Perhaps he spoke louder than he meant to, or perhaps his north-country speech and Galilean tones sounded strange in that company. Conversation stopped; heads turned in his direction.

One of the servants who had been with the soldiers to Gethsemane peered closely at Peter and said firmly, 'Didn't I see you in the garden with him?'

And again Peter denied it, cursing and swearing: 'I tell you, I don't know the man.'

Taken aback by his violence, the man fell silent; and in the silence, clear but distant, came the first cockcrow of a new dawn. The words of Jesus flashed back into Peter's mind: 'Before the cock crows you will disown me three times.' Peter turned on his heel and left the courtyard: and once outside, alone in the cold and dark of the deserted streets, he wept.

From Matthew's Gospel, chapter 26,
Luke's Gospel, chapter 22, John's Gospel, chapter 18

37

Man of Sorrows

Dawn was breaking over Jerusalem. All night in the palace of Caiaphas the priests and religious leaders had been at work, planning how they might have Jesus put to death. He was too popular for their liking; too many people listened to his teaching. The Chief Priests did not understand what he was saying or who he was; and because of this they hated him and were afraid. The safest way out, they thought in their hearts, was to have the fellow silenced- once and for all.

After a sleepless night, his hands tied fast behind him, Jesus was hurried through the empty streets, still cool and shadowless in the grey dawn. They took him first to a meeting of the Jewish Council; and then to the palace of the Roman Governor, whose name was Pontius Pilate.

Meanwhile, Judas Iscariot, who had betrayed Jesus in the darkness of Gethsemane only a few hours before, began to realize what he had done. When he discovered that Jesus, his

friend and Master for so long, was a prisoner before the Governor and likely to be put to death, he was bitterly sorry. He ran to the temple and asked the Chief Priests to take back the thirty pieces of silver money they had paid him.

'I have brought an innocent man to his death,' said Judas.

'That's your affair,' they answered.

Judas flung the coins from him, to scatter on the marble floor, and in his misery went out and hanged himself.

Jesus was standing, still bound, in the judgment hall when Pontius Pilate came out to question him. The priests were there, loud in their accusations that Jesus had spoken against God, and claimed to be a king, and stirred up trouble in the city. Pilate asked many questions; but Jesus stood silent before him. He would say nothing at all.

When Pilate heard that Jesus was from Galilee, he sent him to Prince Herod, the ruler of Galilee, who happened to be staying in Jerusalem; but Jesus would say nothing to Herod either.

And still the Chief Priests spoke angrily against him, trying to get Pilate to condemn him to death.

By this time a crowd had gathered outside Pilate's palace; and encouraged by the priests they too began to shout for Jesus to be killed. In those days criminals were executed by nailing their hands and feet to a wooden cross stuck upright in the ground, and leaving them there for all to see. It was called crucifixion, and it was a cruel way to die.

Pontius Pilate questioned Jesus again. He did not believe that Jesus had done wrong; but beneath his windows the crowd was growing larger.

'Crucify him!' they shouted. 'Crucify! crucify!'

'Shall I crucify your king?' Pilate asked the crowd.

'We have no king but Caesar!' they shouted back.

Pilate looked from the crowd to Jesus, and from Jesus to the crowd. He could not make up his mind. Suddenly he sat down and called for a bowl of water and washed his hands.

'My hands are clean of this man's blood,' he said to the crowd. 'I take no responsibility for his death. You must see to it yourselves.'

So the soldiers took Jesus away. They beat him and jeered at him. The priests had said that he claimed to be a king, so the soldiers gave him a robe and a crown. The robe was of royal purple, old and torn; and the crown woven out of sharp thorn-twigs pressed down upon his head. They put a stick in his hand as a sceptre, and pretended to do him homage.

'Hail, your majesty,' they said to him, spitting on him, and making cruel fun of him.

And then it was time to go. Someone brought the heavy wooden cross and laid it on Jesus' shoulder for him to carry it. Then they opened the gates of the palace and led him out to be crucified.

From Matthew's Gospel, chapter 27,

Luke's Gospel, chapter 23, John's Gospel, chapters 18 and 19

38

The Hill called Calvary

By now it was nine o'clock. The streets were full of people. It was a holiday in Jerusalem and a bright fine morning.

Three prisoners were to be crucified that day, Jesus and two thieves. The Roman soldiers led them in a grim procession from the Governor's palace to the city gates. There they met an African, Simon, making his way toward Jerusalem; and the soldiers stopped him and ordered him to follow them, and to carry the heavy cross in place of Jesus.

So they came to a low hill not far from the city, a hill called Calvary. Here they crucified Jesus, and the two criminals one on either side.

'Father, forgive them,' said Jesus in his pain. 'They do not know what they are doing.'

Quite a crowd of sightseers had followed the soldiers up the hillside. They stood and stared as Jesus hung helpless on the great wooden cross.

Some of them jeered at him. 'He saved others,' they said. 'Now let him save himself. Let him now come down from the cross, and then we will believe him.'

One of the thieves crucified with Jesus turned his head and spoke to him in much the same way.

'Aren't you God's chosen one?' he asked. 'Why don't you save yourself – and us?'

But at that the other thief joined in, saying to his fellow-criminal: 'Have

you no fear of God? It's fair enough for us, we have only got what we deserve, but this man has done nothing wrong.' And to Jesus he said, 'Remember me, when you come into your kingdom.'

'I tell you truly,' said Jesus, 'this very day you will be with me in paradise.'

So the long hours dragged by, and toward noon the day changed. Clouds gathered, the sun was hidden, and it grew strangely dark. Presently through the gloom Jesus gave a great cry: 'My God, my God, why did you forsake me?'

Later he cried again: 'It is finished!' and, 'Father, into your hands I commend my spirit.'

And with these words he died.

In the Temple, the great curtain in the sanctuary split in two from the top to the bottom. The whole earth shook in the darkness, and the rocks split and graves opened.

On the hill of Calvary a Roman centurion was in charge of the soldiers. He had watched Jesus since early morning, and now saw the earthquake and the dark. He peered towards the middle cross, and the still figure hanging there.

'Truly,' said the centurion, 'truly, this man was a Son of God.'

From Matthew's Gospel, chapter 27, Mark's Gospel, chapter 15, Luke's Gospel, chapter 23, John's Gospel, chapter 19

39

Joseph's Garden

The messenger ran lightly along the gallery, slipped between the great pillars, and bowed low before Pontius Pilate, the Governor.

'A visitor to see your Excellency,' he said. 'He gives his name as Joseph of Arimathea. He says he has come about the man named Jesus.'

Presently Joseph was shown into the Governor's presence, and explained the purpose of his visit. The next day was the Jewish Sabbath when no work could be done. So Joseph had come now, in haste, before the Sabbath began, asking to be allowed to take the body of Jesus and to give it a decent burial.

Joseph of Arimathea was a wealthy man, well known in Jerusalem and a member of the Jewish Council. Pontius Pilate called for a soldier to confirm that Jesus was already dead. In fact the soldiers had made sure of this by thrusting a spear into his side. Pilate then gave Joseph permission to take down the body and bury it.

Quickly Joseph and his friend Nicodemus (that same Nicodemus who had once come secretly by night to talk with Jesus) made their way out of the city gate, and up the hill Calvary. The crowd had left long since, frightened by the darkness and the earthquake; and wanting to get ready for the Sabbath tomorrow. Gently and reverently the two men lifted the body down from the cross and laid it on the grass. There they wrapped it in a clean linen cloth,

brought with them for the purpose.

Nearby, as it happened, Joseph had a private garden in which there was a new tomb, never used, cut like a cave from the solid rock, quiet and cool. To this garden Joseph and Nicodemus carried Jesus' body, accompanied by some of the faithful women who had come with him from Galilee. Gently they laid him on a kind of shelf within the rock-hewn tomb, his body wrapped around with sweet-smelling spices in the linen cloth. Then they rolled a great round stone across the entrance to close the tomb: and for the moment there was nothing more they could do. It was already the eve of the Sabbath. By Jewish law nothing further was allowed by way of burial that evening, nor all the next day.

Joseph and Nicodemus and the women stood for a moment, looking at the great stone across the doorway, and remembering Jesus whom they loved. Then, in silence, they made their sad way home.

Early the next morning Pontius Pilate, the Governor, had more visitors. The Chief Priests and the Pharisees came urgently to see him.

'Your Excellency,' they said. 'we recall how that impostor Jesus said while was still alive, "After three days I shall rise again". So will you give orders for the grave to be closely guarded until the third day? Otherwise his disciples may come and steal the body, and then tell the

people that he has been raised from the dead.'

Pilate listened carefully to what they had to say. He was not impressed with these Chief Priests, who had worked so hard to bring about the death of that strange man Jesus. But it was best to be careful.

'You have your guard,' he said to them. 'Go and make it as secure as you can.'

So the Priests and Pharisees went at once to Joseph's garden. They put a seal on the stone across the doorway to the tomb; and left soldiers on watch until daybreak, with orders to guard it well. Then, confident that they had heard the last of this troublesome Jesus, they made their way back into Jerusalem to rest on the Sabbath.

From Matthew's Gospel, chapter 27,
Luke's Gospel, chapter 23, John's Gospel, chapter 19

40

Easter Dawn

From her bed, Mary could just make out the shape of the window, a grey square in the darkness of the room. Through that window there now came the sound of the first cock crowing in Jerusalem, telling her that it was nearly dawn. She had slept little; but quickly she dressed and slipped out into the empty street, a heavy basket of spices in her hand.

The street was not quite empty. Another Mary, Mary of Magdala, was waiting for her, a grey shadow by the doorway. Together they set off for Joseph's garden to finish the work that the Sabbath had interrupted, preparing the body of Jesus for final burial.

By the time they reached the city gate the sky was light with coming dawn. They met no one; and this worried them, for they remembered the great round stone across the doorway of the tomb. It needed strong men to shift that. Who would they find about so early to roll it aside and let them in?

They passed through the gate of the

city and came at last to Joseph's garden. As they reached it the first bright shaft of sunlight told them that day had really dawned – the third day, according to their way of counting, since Jesus had been put to death. And look! Dark against the hillside was the mouth of the tomb; not closed as they had left it, but open, with the stone rolled to one side.

The two women glanced at one another, alarmed and anxious, and after a moment's hesitation, passed inside the tomb. There was the linen cloth; and a rolled-up napkin that had been wrapped around his head; but otherwise the tomb was empty. The body had gone.

They learned later that much earlier, while they were still sleeping, the angel of the Lord had come from heaven to the tomb where Jesus had been buried. While the earth shook beneath him, the angel had rolled back the stone and sat upon it. The seal was broken, the watching soldiers terrified. At first the soldiers were struck to the ground like dead men. Later, hiding their eyes, they took to their heels and ran from the presence of the angel, back toward the city.

The angel was still there when the women came. They caught sight of him – a young man, his face radiant, dressed in a white robe – almost as soon as they had seen the tomb was empty.

'Do not be afraid,' said the angel. 'I know that you are looking for Jesus who was crucified. He is not here – he has risen, just as he said he would. Remember what he told you when he was still in Galilee – that the Son of Man must be betrayed into the hands of sinful men, and must be crucified, and must rise again the third day.'

And as the angel spoke, the women did remember.

'Go quickly,' went on the angel, 'and tell his disciples that he has risen from the dead. He is going on ahead of you to Galilee; there you will see him.'

The women turned, half joyful, half afraid, and ran as fast as they could toward Jerusalem, to give this – the most wonderful news they could have imagined – to Peter and the others.

The words of the angel were ringing in their ears as they raced homeward through that Easter dawn: 'He is not here – he has risen, he has risen, he has risen – just as he said he would.'

From Matthew's Gospel, chapter 28, Mark's Gospel, chapter 16, Luke's Gospel, chapter 24, John's Gospel, chapter 20

41

To Emmaus and Back Again

Cleopas sniffed the country air. He and his companion, both disciples of Jesus, were walking steadily. It was good to be out of Jerusalem that sad Sunday afternoon. All the friends of Jesus were still shaken and desolate after what had happened. It was all done so quickly – the betrayal, the midnight trial, the cruel death. They had talked of nothing else all that weekend; and in twos and threes together had tried to comfort one another now that their Master had gone and all their hopes had come to nothing.

Early that same morning the women had found the tomb open and empty, and said that an angel had told them that Jesus was risen from the dead. But no one knew whether it was true or not. No one knew what to believe.

Cleopas and his friend had left the city by the Western Gate and followed the Roman road. Now as they looked back Jerusalem lay below them in the distance, four or five miles behind. Presently they turned aside from the main road, to take the track up the valley. This was the best part of their journey; the valley lay green and still in the warm sunlight, bright and scented with orange groves and gardens.

Others passed them from time to time, chatting about their families and their business affairs. But Cleopas and his friend had only one thing to talk about. Their heavy hearts brought them over and over again to talk of Jesus and what might have been; and why God had allowed him to die so horribly and so young.

About a mile from the village they were going to – a place called Emmaus – two roads met. As the companions walked steadily on, deep in talk, another man fell into step beside them. He asked them what it was they were discussing that made them look so sad.

Cleopas turned to him in astonishment: 'You must be the only person staying in Jerusalem who hasn't heard all the things that have happened there recently,' he said.

'What things?' asked the stranger.

'Oh,' said Cleopas. 'All about Jesus, from Nazareth – a prophet strong in what he did and what he said, in God's eyes as well as the people's. Haven't you heard how our Chief Priests and rulers handed him over for execution and had him crucified? But we were hoping he was the one who was to come and set Israel free . . .' And they went on to tell the stranger of the empty tomb.

Then it was his turn to speak.

'Aren't you failing to understand?' he said to them, 'and slow to believe in all that the prophets have said? Was not Christ bound to suffer like this, and so find his glory?' And he began to explain to them the teaching of the Scriptures.

By now they were at Emmaus, and Cleopas stopped outside the house where he was to stay. The stranger was about to walk on, but they persuaded him to join them – it was already nearly evening – and so the three of them went in to supper.

There, at the table, the stranger took the loaf, gave thanks, and broke the bread in his hands, and passed it to them. And in that moment they recognized him. Suddenly, and beyond all doubt, they knew that it was Jesus. And even as they knew him, he vanished and was gone.

The friends looked at one another, their eyes wide in wonder.

'Did we not feel our hearts on fire as he talked with us on the road and explained the Scriptures to us?' they said.

They left their supper and hurried back, seven miles in the growing dark. The stars were shining as they reached Jerusalem.

From Luke's Gospel, chapter 24

42

'Peace be to you all!'

'Who is it?' a voice asked sharply, as Cleopas knocked a second time on the bolted door. He and his friend had hurried back to Jerusalem, too excited to be tired or hungry, bursting to tell the other disciples that Jesus had talked with them on the road to Emmaus. They had made their way through the darkened streets to the house where the disciples were meeting. Inside they could hear many voices, but the door was locked. Cleopas knocked loudly: and the voices ceased abruptly, cut off in mid-sentence. He knocked again.

'Who is it?' said the voice.
'Cleopas,' he replied.
'Just a moment.'
There was the sound of bolts being drawn back, and the door opened on the crowded room. Ten of the disciples were there and many other friends of Jesus. They were meeting behind locked doors for fear of the Jews and the Chief Priests.

Before Cleopas could speak, they burst out with their own exciting news. 'It is true!' they told him. 'The

Lord has really risen – he has appeared to Simon.'

And then Cleopas and his companion told the story of their walk: how they too had seen the Lord and spoken with him; and how they had recognized him when he broke the loaf at supper.

They were all still talking excitedly together when suddenly Jesus himself stood there among them in the room.

'Peace be to you all!' he said.

For a moment they were terrified. They shrank back, thinking it must be a ghost. But Jesus spoke to them again.

'Why are you so worried?' he asked. 'Look at my hands and my feet – it is really I myself! Feel me and see; ghosts have no flesh and bones as you can see that I have.'

Overwhelmed with joy, the

disciples still could not quite believe it, so Jesus asked them if they had anything to eat. The remains of a meal were on the table, and they found him a piece of fish, and watched him as he ate.

Then he spoke to them again, saying, 'Peace be unto you all! As the Father sent me, so I send you.' And he breathed on them, saying, 'Receive the Holy Spirit!'

Now it happened that Thomas was not with the others that Sunday evening. Through the next week the other disciples kept on telling him, 'We have seen the Lord,' but he would not believe it.

'Unless I see in his own hand the mark of the nails,' Thomas told them, 'and put my finger where the nails were and put my hand into his side, I will never believe.'

And from this they could not move him.

A week later the disciples were again all together, with the doors shut. Thomas was among them this time, when Jesus came to them again.

'Peace be with you,' said Jesus; and turned at once to Thomas.

'Put your finger here,' he said. 'Look, here are my hands. Take your hand and put it into my side. You must not doubt but believe.'

Thomas looked at Jesus, and was sure beyond any doubting. 'My Lord and my God,' he said.

'Is it because you have seen me that you believe?' Jesus said to him gently. 'Happy are those who have never seen me and yet have believed!'

From Luke's Gospel, chapter 24, John's Gospel, chapter 20

43

The Figure on the Shore

It had been a disappointing night's work. Peter and James and John, all fishermen from Galilee, were back for the moment at their old trade. On that first Easter morning, Jesus had sent word to Peter that he would come to them in Galilee; and so they waited, by the very lakeside where they first met him, until he should come.

Last evening, with four other disciples, they had taken one of the boats and fished steadily, up and down the dark water, from dusk to dawn – and caught nothing at all. Their old skill, hardly used for the last three busy years with Jesus, seemed to have deserted them.

The stars had gone: and in the grey light of early dawn they rowed back, disappointed, toward the empty beach. But it was not quite deserted, for well before they reached it a lone figure hailed them. His voice carried to them clearly over the calm water:

'Have you caught anything?'

'No,' they shouted back.

'Throw the net to starboard,' came the reply, 'and you'll have a catch.'

They had nothing to lose, so for one more time they threw out the net and began to haul. Before it even reached the side of the boat they could tell they had a record catch.

'All together, heave!' someone shouted, and they bent their broad backs to haul the net aboard; but it was too full of fish for them to lift. (When they counted them later, they found a hundred and fifty-three!)

John – perceptive John – stared in the growing light of morning at the figure on the shore. He turned to Peter, saying, 'It is the Lord!'

Peter – impulsive Peter – pulled his coat about him and plunged overboard to swim the hundred yards to land. The others followed in the boat, towing the net full of fish.

On the beach a small fire was burning with a fish cooking on the charcoal, and a loaf of bread. What passed between Jesus (for it *was* Jesus) and Peter is not for us to know. It was their first talk alone together since that cock-crow in the palace of Caiaphas. Perhaps they had no need of words.

When the boat was beached, the

keel grating on the shingle, Jesus told them to bring some of the catch and to come and have breakfast. In that spring dawn, with the sun rising and the world newmade, they sat down together on the beach. The hills were green in the early sunshine; the water lapped gently on the shore nearby; Jesus was back among them and they were entirely happy.

After breakfast Jesus turned to Peter. 'Simon, son of John,' he said, 'do you love me more than these?'

'Yes, Lord,' said Peter. 'You know I love you.'

'Then feed my lambs,' said Jesus.

Three times Jesus asked Peter this question; and told him to feed his lambs and tend his sheep. Peter was

forgiven, fully and freely. The terrible moment of cock-crow in Jerusalem was behind him. Jesus was giving him a new work to do. Peter's strength and courage, his repentance and forgiveness – and all he had heard of Jesus' teaching – were helping to make of him the Rock (that is what the name 'Peter' really means) on which the risen Lord Jesus would build his worldwide church.

So, together, Master and disciple walked in the sunlight by the water's edge. For Peter and the others the long night was over. Morning had come again.

From John's Gospel, chapter 21

44

'To the Ends of the Earth

Nearly six weeks had passed since that first Easter Day when Jesus rose from the dead. Jesus had been seen by many people. He had been seen by his friends (never by his enemies) both in and around Jerusalem, and away in Galilee. Only six weeks ago the disciples thought they had lost him for ever; the stone had been rolled right across the doorway to close the tomb in which his body lay. Three days later, with mounting excitement, they knew beyond doubt that he was alive! On the hill called Calvary he had finished the work he came to do, to save people everywhere from their sins. By his resurrection from the tomb in Joseph's garden he had conquered all the powers of death.

The disciples knew that very soon now they must lose him a second time. But this time, not to a cross and grave; but to his heavenly home, and to his Father's throne of majesty on high. Over the last weeks, Jesus had been preparing them and teaching them; promising to send his Holy Spirit to stay with them for ever; and assuring them that he himself would still be with them, though they would not see him.

So the day came when he talked for the last time with the eleven disciples, and promised them God's special power for the work they were to do.

'You shall be witnesses for me,' he told them, 'in Jerusalem, and all over Judea and Samaria, and away to the ends of the earth. And mark this, I am sending you my Father's promised gift: so stay here in this city until you receive the special power God will give you.'

With that, he led them out toward Bethany along a road they well remembered. Two months before he had ridden the colt down this dusty track, the cheers of the people ringing in their ears, the palm branches waving in the sunlight. Now, unnoticed and alone as they retraced their steps, the disciples saw him not as King of the Jews only, but as the King of Kings. They halted on the mountainside, where no other eyes could see, and Jesus looked around at the eleven familiar weatherbeaten faces, and lifted up his hands and blessed them. Then, while they watched, he was taken up toward heaven, until a cloud hid him from their eyes.

For a while no one moved. It seemed, sadly, that this really was goodbye. Until suddenly beside the eleven disciples there appeared two men dressed in white who said to them: 'Men of Galilee, why are you standing here, looking up into the sky? This same Jesus who has been taken up from you into heaven will come back in the same way as you have seen him go.'

So at last for the moment there was nothing more to be done. The disciples turned to make their way back to the city. They remembered

what he had said about being his
witnesses, about the promise of the
Holy Spirit and power from on high,
about how he had told them, 'I am
with you always, even to the end of
the world.'

And suddenly they were happy
men. They returned to Jerusalem
with great joy, and were often in the
Temple, praising and blessing God.
Soon the day came, as Jesus had
promised, when they began their new
work as witnesses for him.

But that is the start of another story.
You and I are part of that story here in
our world today: and no one can tell
when it will finish.

From Matthew's Gospel, chapter 28, Luke's Gospel, chapter 24,

the Acts of the Apostles, chapter 1